Programme Notes
Case studies for locating experimental theatre

Published by the
Live Art
Development
Agency

I believe it is essential for the healthy development of any society that its culture is not just led by innovations in the market and particularly its control of financially monopolised areas – such as the market control of new technologies – but rather that it continues to refine its vital human communication. This crucial exchange must be radical, unexpected, or previously unknown to truly move us forward. For me, this is the role of experimental theatre.
Robert Pacitti, Artistic Director, Pacitti Company

Programme Notes is about furthering dialogues and collaborations between the theatrical mainstream and artists from the independent sector.

Over the last decade or so there has been a growing sense that artistic directors and programmers across the UK are expressing greater interest in work that pushes at the edges of our expectations of what theatre could be. Some venues are actively programming experimental works. Others are expressing a keenness to explore the opportunities for taking their audiences on new journeys. Whilst it is acknowledged that this work is challenging, sometimes difficult, often compelling and engaging, it is also work that can attract new audiences, offer new experiences, and add bold new strands to a venue's programme. Whether it is the National Theatre collaborating with Shunt, Duckie's events at the Barbican, Noble & Silver at Soho Theatre, or Gob Squad working on the main stage of Nottingham Playhouse it is increasingly evident that theatres in the UK are excited about a new set of relationships with experimental artists and companies.

And more and more experimental companies themselves are interested in changing and innovating in different contexts. No longer content to occupy only studio theatres, site specific locations, or 'the fringes' of our culture, many of today's artists are equally excited by the possibilities of working in main houses and on centre stages, thinking anew about the kinds of roles they can play, the kinds of audiences they can talk to, and the kinds of stories they can tell them.

There has perhaps never been a better time to progress the place and profile of independent theatre makers in the UK, or for our theatre venues to take a fresh look at what they can do, and how they can do it.

So, how can more theatre venues and experimental companies respond to such shifts in the theatrical landscape of the UK and invest in the cultural future? How can theatres that are intrigued by the possibilities of new theatrical forms and new relationships with audiences be encouraged to not only take more risks but be better equipped to do so?

Programme Notes has been created as a resource to contribute to these debates and stimulate interest by reflecting models of exciting and innovative relationships at work in different places in the UK.

In a series of commissioned case studies and essays, leading artists, producers, and commentators have been invited to consider the nature, breadth and value of contemporary theatre practices, and to write about specific projects from their own experiences and perspectives, providing practical insights into programming initiatives and audience development work that have connected the mainstream with experimental theatre.

In the introductory essays for *Programme Notes*, theatre critic Lyn Gardner writes about the tidal wave of new theatre practices and their exciting relationships with audiences in the UK, suggesting that 'perhaps not since the late 1960s has Britain's theatre culture been quite so fluid, quite so open to the possibilities of the new'; whilst the writer and director Tim Etchells talks about the potential of contemporary theatre to connect with its audiences in previously unimagined ways: its capacity 'to pick people up and really take them places'. The case studies and interviews provide a fascinating understanding of different approaches to developing new ways of working within more theatres, arts centres and festivals in the UK.

Programme Notes is concerned with how theatres might shift their programmes and, in doing so, their audiences. This short selection of essays and interviews asks how theatres might alter their artistic aspirations through new approaches and in dialogue with a different range of artists and theatre makers.

Programme Notes is a handbook for artists and commentators, and indeed anyone interested in theatre in the UK today. But it is especially a resource for theatre programmers, artistic directors and venue managers, with the aim of sharing knowledge and stimulating thinking around a broader range of new and emergent theatrical practices.

Lois Keidan and Daniel Brine, Live Art Development Agency.
David Micklem, Arts Council England.

There is something stirring

Lyn Gardner

There is something stirring. A huge mechanical elephant comes to London and up to a million people come out onto the streets to play and laugh and wonder, the numbers swelled not by reviews in the broadsheet papers, but by word of mouth and hundreds of thousands of images sent by the camera phone – that modern, technological Pied Piper. At the Barbican, Bobby Baker sells out the main auditorium and is invited back again. Forced Entertainment – ignored for years by the mainstream – suddenly attracts glowing reviews and is discovered and feted by a whole new generation of theatre-goers, many of whom weren't even born when the company was founded. The Fierce Festival in Birmingham and the National Review of Live Art in Glasgow offer audiences – hungry for a theatre experience which doesn't just pin them like butterflies on a plush red velvet seat – a taste of something very different. The British Council champion and send abroad as cultural ambassadors a raft of companies and live artists who most first string theatre critics in this country won't even have heard of, let alone seen.

Yes, there is undoubtedly a shift going on. Perhaps not since the late 1960s has Britain's theatre culture been quite so fluid, quite so open to the possibilities of the new and more willing to break the rules set by a theatre establishment that still clings to late 19th and early 20th century notions of theatre practice, like a bedraggled shipwreck survivor clinging to a rotting plank of wood. We have lived too long in a theatre culture in which the past is valued over the future, the classic over the contemporary, and where the point of reference is John Osborne, David Hare and Tom Stoppard rather than Impact, Welfare State International and Pip Simmons. This is a world where Stanislavsky has been celebrated and Artaud ignored.

But there are signs that the dominance is being broken. If the mid 1990s were seen as golden age in playwrighting with the emergence of new voices such as Sarah Kane and Mark Ravenhill, the early part of the 21st century has been a similarly revolutionary time in theatre's search for form and a new relationship between performer and audience. The outside has suddenly become the inside, and the fringe is infiltrating the mainstream on a scale not previously seen or even imagined.

Companies such as Shunt and Punchdrunk have been taken by the National Theatre; puppetry embraced by the RSC, burlesque by the Barbican. In London, the Chelsea Theatre reinvents itself as a live art venue and Home has people knocking on its door eager to engage with the intimacies of performance in a room in a family house rather than a theatre. In Sheffield, shows such as Shadowmouth – a collaboration between writer Meredith Oakes and director/ choreographer Dominic Leclerc – are part of a growing and increasingly important strand of work in which neither the word nor the physical has the upper hand. The theatre of transgression has entered the mainstream via the craze for burlesque, and the work of Duckie and individual artists such as Ursula Martinez are taking live art practice to audiences who may not know what the term 'live art' means but who certainly like what they see. In the capital, young companies are deserting traditional pub theatres for found spaces – derelict warehouses and factories, church crypts, and on the Edinburgh fringe – that most commercial of market places – the most successful new venue of recent years has been Aurora Nova @ St Stephens, where European companies such as Derevo and Fabrik have found not just a home but a devoted audience.

What we are seeing is a movement which has the potential to put theatre and live art right at the centre of our culture as it breaks down all the old divisions and suspicions between theatre and live art, the playhouse and the gallery, the text and the visual and physical. One of the joys of a piece such as Marisa Carnesky's *Ghost Train* – played out on a purpose built fairground ride – is the fact that it cannot be classified because it breaks all the rules and defies all expectation. It is its very 'differentness' which distinguishes it, as much as its sexual politics and its games with high and low art. It is its 'differentness' that also lends it an accessibility and diversity. Unlike traditional theatre which takes place behind the closed doors of the playhouse, it shuts nobody out, and it allows the audience to take themselves to the event. It has a plasticity which ensures that it is what every individual member of the audience thinks it is. Similarly the *Sultan's Elephant* could be read in many ways, not least as an artistic occupation of the streets, an invasion that disrupts the spectacle of everyday life and reclaims the streets of the city as a place that belongs to us and where we can play and dream. This is art which allows us ownership of our own lives and own imaginative processes.

The thing that makes this surge of interest in 'differentness' and experiment particularly encouraging is that it appears to be driven by audiences rather than by critics, commentators or even venues. We all lag far behind. We live in a world which is becoming increasingly homogenous, where one high street in one town looks very much like a high street in one several hundred miles away and a cup of coffee bought in Newcastle tastes just like one bought in Truro. It is a place where one Hollywood blockbuster has the same special effects and looks pretty much like another Hollywood blockbuster. Novels and plays are often sold on the premise that if you like this, you will also like that because after all one piece of chick lit is pretty much like another and if you liked Art you will certainly like Heroes.

Yet increasingly it seems to me that audiences see through these marketing scams and hunger for cultural experiences which not only are different but which have an authenticity. They crave the intimacy and emotional connectedness that live art can deliver, but which is mostly absent from the traditional well made play produced in a Victorian playhouse where from the back row of the stalls everyone on stage looks Lilliputian. How can such an experience compete with the intimacy of Kira O'Reilly's encounters at the National Review of Live Art in which she invited audience members to either cut her or hold her? The audience is no longer merely a passive spectator, they are part of the event itself. They make it, alongside the artist, and every performance is unique because the participants are always different. And it is not just one to one performances that work on this premise – a piece such as Robert Pacitti's *A Forest*, doesn't just perform to its audience, it implicates us by bringing us into the circle and making us voice our innermost secrets and longings.

It is clear that such encounters are addictive. The scripted play seems tame once the audience has tasted this power and the possibility of interaction. We are no longer content to sit quietly in our seats when we can storm the stages. Once we have learned this new theatrical vocabulary, we want more opportunities to hear it and speak it, we no longer find it satisfying merely to stick to other people's scripts. What's more, there are many more people who are comfortable with this new theatrical language. The rise of the Theatre Studies A Level that gives as much weight to the work of the David Glass Ensemble and Forced Entertainment as it does to the well-made play is creating a new generation of theatre goers and theatre-makers who are at home with experimentation, the devised, the physical and the visual and who instinctively understand the connections between a theatre tradition and a gallery tradition. Many of these young people are going on to degree courses in advanced theatre practice and creating a substantial wave of new practitioners who don't want to make drama but who do want to make theatre, who couldn't care less about plays but who care very passionately about live art.

This is potentially a brave new world in which we live, made all the more exciting by the rise of a new generation of creative producers who eschew traditional theatre and are forging new partnerships and ways of working that encompass live art and work in non-theatre spaces. It is a welcome sign that even Nicolas Hytner, artistic director of that bastion of the theatre establishment, the National Theatre, is far less afraid than his predecessors of the new, the experimental and transgressive and has been spotted checking out Duckie as well as the latest play at the Royal Court.

Even so, I am afraid. Audiences and these new producers are often far braver than the programmers, funders and critics, and we have also been here before: after all this is not the first time that an alternative theatre and live art culture has flourished. The late Sixties and Seventies saw a flowering of companies and individual artists who eschewed traditional theatre for more experimental modes, and even in the 1980s – supported largely by the ICA and a radical arts centre tradition – companies were still being founded to explore new theatrical languages. With the glorious exception of Forced Entertainment, regarded by many in Europe and the US as *the* great British theatre company of the last 30 years, there have been few survivors. Perhaps it was not surprising, after all that was an era when those who ran our theatres and most critics came from a Leavis tradition which values the literary and the literal over the language of dreams and ritual and the personal story and experience. As David Glass has observed, the history of theatre is written by the victors, and the victors have always been the text-based play, the writer and the director who realises the writer's vision. Some of the innovations have been integrated – at least superficially – into the mainstream, but most of it has disappeared and along with it the traditions and teachers who could hand down the expertise. It means that each new generation of theatrical experimenters has had to reinvent the wheel all over again.

The difference this time is the sheer scale of what is happening. When up to a million people spontaneously take to the streets to watch the *Sultan's Elephant*, or you see people besieging the box office at Aurora Nova hoping to get a ticket to see Derevo and Duckie sells out at the Barbican, you know that this time change is really possible, and that we can create a bolder, broader and more invigorating and inclusive culture in which theatre and live art have a central place. The audiences are already storming the barricades, it is up to the rest of us to give them a helping hand because the revolution has already started without us, and it would be such a pity to miss it.

Lyn Gardner writes about theatre for The Guardian. Her first novel Into the Woods is published by David Fickling

All Graeae's work is intrinsically experimental
theatre. Experimental theatre in the UK is seen
as a dare or a risk. All creative endeavour is a
risk with experimentation as the heart beat.
This gives artists the adrenalin to cut the edges
of anal traditionalism. UK artists rely on this
buzz because lets face it not all of us are in it
for the money! Experimental theatre needs to be
embraced and not seen as something that only
resides within college walls otherwise our
theatrical climate will continue to be a series of
white middleclass kitchen sink dramas playing
to the same audiences forever and ever.

Jenny Sealey, Artistic Director,
Graeae Theatre Company

Some people do something.

The others watch, listen, try to be there.

Tim Etchells

There's a word for people like you....
...and that word is... Audience.

Says Richard Lowdon directly addressing
those who are watching him near the start
of our 1996 performance *Showtime*.
An audience..., he adds later in the same
piece, with much the same attitude of
comical menace and accusation *...likes to sit
in the dark, and watch other people DO IT.*

This much at least I guess we can count on.

But for the rest it's perhaps for the good that we can't count on much at all.

Theatre and performance are for me best seen as spaces of possibility – places where anything can and should happen. After naturalism, after Brecht, after the absurd, after Kitchen Sink and musicals, after collaborative this and experimental that, after the multi-disciplinary high-and-low-budget, high-and-low-brow extravaganzas, after empty spaces and physical theatres and all that very visual theatre and all that theatre that is also installation and all the performance theatre and the dance drama and the dance theatre and the loud music and the strange slow images and the even-stranger jump-cut images, the re-definition of mime to include talking and the reinvention of dance to more-or-less exclude dancing as such, after all of it, after the fragmentation and the swearing, after the violence and the microphones and the yelling and after the reading and the formal shock horror, after the content *scandale* and the buggery, the no-star reviews and the cacophony of tipping seats, after all that 'is-it-really-acting' and 'is-it-really-theatre' and 'is-it-really-art' etc etc etc perhaps we can say now, finally, that theatre can be what we want and need it to be in order to meet audiences and look them straight in the eyes with a question and an attempt to talk about what its like to live in this world now. After all that perhaps we can just say that the door is open. That the space is one of possibility – that anything can happen in the next one hour and 45 minutes, that no one needs permission from a parent or guardian or the approval of a responsible adult, the mayor, the Lord Chamberlain or the Ghosts of Shakespeare, Osbourne or any living dead critics from any national newspapers, I mention no names. The door is open. Anything is possible. All of the above, and anything more (or less) or anything totally different that anyone feels inspired, inclined or compelled to bring to the table, to the stage. That's all that anyone ever wanted after all; that the door be open and left that way so that more people can get their foot through it, artists and audiences.

So let's do the basics one more time. What are the rules of theatre?

Some people do something. The others watch, listen, try to be there.

Anything else we need to know?

Not really, no.

Are we talking about that old punk adage 'here are three chords now form a band'?

We could be. Or it could be way way more complicated than that. The door is open.

Are we talking about Jasper Johns' three part instructions piece?

*"Take an object.
Do something to it.
Do something else to it".*

Sounds good to me. The door is open.

What excites me is work in theatre and performance that makes contact. It might pick people up and really take them places – temporarily making different worlds or states-of-mind, pulling spectators into new landscapes, or incisive re-mixed versions of our own. Or it might just pass on the chance to summon an elsewhere (real or imagined), and take the time instead to draw the people watching into a kind of long and deep look at themselves, even as they sit there in their seats. Either way there's something bold and direct in the work I love, a simplicity and strength that doesn't compromise or contradict it's many other much more ephemeral qualities, like risk or fragility or playfulness.

Perhaps the work I see which excites me most combines the approaches above – slipping and sliding between the act of

summoning – a story, a world, some figures/'characters', a landscape, a set of concerns – and the process of holding up a mirror to the space and time of the auditorium, inviting the audience to think about itself, its role and place in the world, its role and place in the rather bizarre event or system that is theatre – that strange practice of sitting together in groups of 50 to 1,000, arranged in darkened rows and watching in relative silence while dances, speeches, dialogues or action take place in an area marked out as a stage.

Watching the best theatre and performance we are together and alone. Together in the sense that we're aware of the temporary and shifting bonds that link us both to the stage and to our fellow watchers, plugged into the group around and in front of us, the communal situation, sensing the laughter, attentiveness, tension or unease that grip us collectively, in waves and ripples, in jolts, jumps and uncertain spirals or in other formations that roll and flicker around auditorium and stage, but do not yet have a name. Sat watching we spread-out, osmose, make connections. But at the same time, even as we do so, we feel our separateness, our difference from those around us, from those on-stage. Even as we shift and flow with the group, we're aware that our place in its emerging consensus, its temporary community, is partial and provisional – that in any case the group itself – there in the theatre, as elsewhere, in our cities and streets, in the relations between nations, peoples and states – is always as much a fraught and necessary question, a longing and a problem, as it is any kind of certainty.

&

Nearly twenty years ago Claire MacDonald wrote that "The media-glutted consumer culture of the city needs a new visual grammar to prise it open" adding that "If radical theatre really has any future it won't be in a worn out social realism..."

You could say the same thing now pretty well. The reality moves on – more digital now, more culturally diverse, more nervous, more networked and somehow even more fractured – and as the reality shifts so too theatre and performance duck, dive, shiver and mutate to keep up, shifting and changing in order to grab something of all that takes place, or to contrast it in just the right way, or just to create a space of reflection or refraction that makes just the right kind of sense, or just the right kind of nonsense, and in either case just the right kind of playful intervention, to be true to or true of the time.

For me the places where the action is are those where the door I mentioned before is most emphatically open – those where artists and theatres, makers and venues of different kinds are taking all kinds of risks, taking all kinds of liberties.

Back when Claire Macdonald wrote that article – when Forced Entertainment was all of two years old – we would certainly have been intimidated by a 500 seat theatre, let alone one that contained an audience with much hint of 'the mainstream'. We'd never played in anything like that big, or to that kind of crowd. In those days the ICA, with its 150 or so seats, and the vast expanse of maybe 7.5m width, seemed enormous, official and public in an almost epic way – we'd never really played there either. But by now you could say that things have changed.

For us things changed at first in mainland Europe. I think that's probably very often the case for British artists making theatre outside of the play-writing tradition. A lot of the breaks and chances come from elsewhere. It would have been in Germany or Belgium or Holland that we first played and got used to playing larger spaces, and where we first encountered the larger audiences whose make-up didn't fit the same demographic as those we played to at home. And afterwards Switzerland, Norway, Italy, France, Canada, America and elsewhere. And somewhere in there things changed in Britain too.

For a long time here, at home, we languished in a strange marginal position. Feeling shut-out of larger spaces, locked out of 'the mainstream' (whatever that might be) and at the same time perhaps rather too bound up with the idea of being 'outside', with a self-imposed role of exile, to do much about it. Its telling that the main thing it took to change this situation was a change in our own approach and in our own ambitions. Encouraged by a few strategic programmers, and by a few people inside the funding system, we took to assuming that doors were (or might be) open instead of closed. We got interested in pursuing a dialogue with larger spaces in the UK, seeking out those meetings and conversations where we could talk through plans and ambitions, with an eye towards finding common ground; looking for crossover. And slowly since then, bit by bit, we have found some, in fact more than we might at first have expected.

I get excited about simplicity. About single ideas taken very very far, about approaches pushed to their very limits.

I love work that plugs into popular culture – work which breathes the same air as the rest of us. I love the way that artists sift through almost discarded OR EVERYDAY things – going back through things that are discredited, abandoned or in some sense marginalised by mainstream OR OFFICIAL culture, or by theatre itself. As if here, in the ruins, in the POPULAR FORMS, in the TRACKS, TRACES and detritus of the everyday (sometimes invisible simply because of a certain ubiquity) there might be clues, truths, possibilities. Vaudeville. Magic Acts. Bollywood. Drag. Bad movies, bad TV. Pop songs. Am Dram. Rock gigs. Pantomime. Computer games. Stand-Up. Line Dancing. Musicals. Comic books. These things and others might be relevant in making a theatre for the twenty-first century. Press conferences, show trials, quiz-shows, chat-shows, public inquiries, panel discussions. These might also be relevant. Drag acts, cabaret, storytelling, channel hopping. These might also be relevant. Performance art, poetry, dance, film and visual art. These things might also be relevant. Don't rule anything out. The streets of the city you live in. The fragment of conversation you overheard in a bar. Something your child or your lover whispered when close to edges of sleep. A mis-heard news broadcast. An internet rumour. The door is open after all and the task at hand is to find a theatre that can speak to audiences of the times in which we live.

I get excited about theatre and performance work that is brave enough to surrender control – trusting its audience to think, trusting that they will go useful places when they're let off the leash of dramaturgical control, or even trusting that a trip through the ostensibly not so useful places (boredom, drifting, free-association) can be more than useful or constructive in the longer run. Trusting audiences, and opening space for them – its more than one kind of door that needs opening after all.

I get excited about laughter – about the way that a whole audience can start heading that way and I get excited about silence too – about the strange stillness that comes over an audience that is – for a moment, or a whole section – puzzled, conflicted or on tenterhooks because somehow the game has been changed. I love the sudden turns that artists make between laughter and something else – the switch between laughter and silence, or between laughter and tears – and the sudden switch back again.

I love work that shifts me again and again from a recognisable territory – I know where I am – into deeper water, into a place where the references or allusions are more dense, more unclear, or where the combination of things is simply too hard to easily make sense of. The defying of expectations. The breaking of frames. The switch. The jump. The crash. The occasion, in any performance, for sudden wonder.

And I love the way that somehow, whatever its landscape, whatever its means that the best in contemporary performance brings me back to the world and a consideration of our place in it. The way that the outside comes in, or the inside comes out, unfolding.

🐾

Or to put that another way.

Inside the theatre there are only the performers and the audience.

Onstage the performers will have some material items – this night's variation on flimsy or not-so-very-flimsy scenery, plus props, costumes and whatever other stuff. The audience, for their part, will most likely have their coats, their handbags and the contents of their pockets. But

that's all – aside from the performers, the audience and the stuff they each have with them that's really all there is. *The whole of the rest of the world* – its physical locations and landscapes, its entire population, its complete set of objects and all of its very very many unfolding events, large and small, significant and banal – is invariably outside this room, this place, *emphatically absent*.

Theatre then must always (?) be: the summoning of presence in the context of absence; a bringing in of the world.

And in the space of this – this space of extreme limitation, this space of absurd, almost impossible constriction – anything is possible.

Back then in 1986, when Claire wrote that article flagging for the one-millionth time the redundancy of a worn-out-realism, the relationship between the mainstream, the literary theatre and the live art/performance scene in the UK looked very oppositional.

I have to say that writing, now in 2006, it sometimes seems as though things did not change so much. Here in the UK we still do rather too much to deserve a reputation for consuming low-grade American cultural waste-product (I'm talking actors and shows but you can easily extend it to politics) and too much to bolster our image as a kind of quaint museum theme-island with Shakespeare as figurehead stood next to those blokes in the funny outfits at the Tower of London, probably encouraging them to read from Hamlet 'just as he first intended it'. Even when things do seem to be moving they don't always move on as much as we'd like to imagine they do. "That British New Writing.." one Flemish Theatre programmer said to me years ago, earnestly puzzled or playing devils advocate "… it's really just the same as the old British writing isn't it?"

Indeed. There are days here when I doubt the depth of the resolve of mainstream theatres to really embrace new approaches, to take bold steps, to really open the door to new work that is produced outside of the literary model, and the new audiences that I think would come with them. And on a larger scale – perhaps more important – there are days when the attitude of suspicion and scepticism in the UK towards art in general – context for the conservatism you can sense in some institutions – gets more than fucking tedious.

But on other days I'm more cheery, though I have to say it's not my natural tendency. I can feel some optimism based on how things already are in mainland Europe, and have been for years, optimism connected to the fact that there is a much greater interplay there between 'experimental' theatre and the mainstream of larger theatres and festivals. I can also feel optimism because of the strength and persistence of the alliances that as a company we have made here, on home turf, and which we've seen other artists make here and there with larger venues around the country. And I have an optimism too which arises from the way that British theatre is of course changing and shifting, not in some monosyllabic way but in fits and starts, eddies and flurries, especially in the work of groups and artists from or at 'the edges', artists who are finding new ways to talk directly and playfully to audiences, new ways to make theatre and performance speak. I have an optimism too from the evidence of our own practice, touring here in the UK – because we've seen many times in different places that when contextualised properly and marketed with the right kinds of intelligence and commitment (and resources!) the kinds of work we make can sit in 'mainstream' venues here, and draw good, hungry and in the end enthusiastic crowds. Its an optimism born from the fact that where we do find partners and build meaningful alliances to present the work (with all the hard work and effort and struggle to find the way that that implies) – in Glasgow, in Warwick, in Sheffield, in Dublin, in Newcastle – that it can and does work. We know this from audiences numbers, from their reactions, from post-show discussions, from the long emails and other communications we get from people following shows.

I think audiences grow around what you do and around what you give them. You get the audience you deserve, or the audience you expect and conservative programming breeds conservative audiences. But from my experience here (and elsewhere) a change of tack can really work. Treat people like they are intelligent, game for anything, able to cope and interested in challenging, funny, bright and contemporary art and they rise to the occasion. There may be some walkouts and some 'no thank-you's' – but there might very may well be along with that, the beginnings of a relationship with a different audience. There are plenty of people to whom the words challenging, experimental, innovative are actually positives, plenty of people to whom the different take on the world that the so-called experimental offers is a highly valued addition to their cultural lives, a useful window on their world. We get to see a lot of them, at gigs, at home and abroad.

I guess I wasn't asked, in writing this introduction, to outline a course of action for experimental theatre and the mainstream – which is just as well since there's too much to be discussed and tussled over before any such thing could really be resolved and in any case I doubt that change really comes from policy – I think it comes from art, and from determined presenters who want to make things happen. But I do think that its important to flag here the need for the funding system to take more active steps to encourage the larger/mainstream venues in the UK to make links with experimental theatre, with artists who are working in different ways, to different agendas. There are plenty of initiatives and alliances already in existence around the country that would benefit from this kind of support and I'm guessing that some financial support might help to make still more things possible – at least in the sense of taking away some of the risk that doing new things seems to engender. I'm wondering too what success in the development of this area would be? I think if we could look at the programmes of middle-scale theatres around the country in five years time and see innovative projects from experimental theatre makers occupying pride of place in the seasons of such venues – not as opportunistic manoeuvres to fill a split week – but as part of a serious and ongoing attempt to open doors to new work and new audiences – then I think we could be sure that the kinds of talks we're having in and around a publication like this one have been worthwhile.

In the meantime of course we'll all just get on with our work, as we always do, venues and artists – making such alliances as we can, finding the best ways to put the strange, darkly comical, ironic, brutal, weirdly entertaining stuff we do in front of audiences because we believe that what we're doing has value and urgency. I'm going to be partisan here as I have been through this writing, not even-handed – I want to say that this work 'outside the mainstream' of which we're just one small part, one tendency in a field of diverse tendencies – this work has for me the most extraordinary capacity to describe, address and engage the contemporary world in vital and vivid terms, and that it reaches audiences with a depth, complexity and clarity that other forms of theatre do rarely these days. Audiences – intelligent, playful, bright and inventive audiences – no matter what you hear to the contrary, are hungry for that. They need and deserve it.

Tim Etchells is an artist and a writer making projects in diverse contexts and media. Best known for his work as director of the Sheffield-based performance ensemble Forced Entertainment, he has also collaborated with a wide range of other artists including Meg Stuart, Vlatka Horvat, Hugo Glendinning and Franko B. His published work includes the collection of writings on and for performance *Certain Fragments* (Routledge, 1999) and *The Dream Dictionary for the Modern Dreamer* (Duckworths, 2001). Recent Forced Entertainment performances include the deconstructed ironic rock spectacle, *Bloody Mess* (2004) and *Exquisite Pain* (2005) based on a text by the French conceptual artist Sophie Calle. The group's most recent work is titled *The World In Pictures* and premiered in May 2006. Etchells is currently a Creative Fellow in the Department of Theatre Studies at Lancaster University.
www.forcedentertainment.com

Bringing Glamour To The Masses; The Lyric Hammersmith 1994-2004

Neil Bartlett

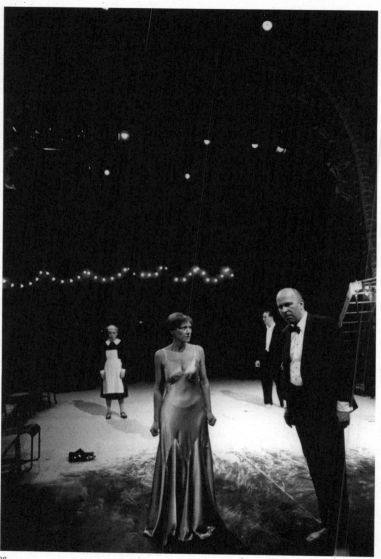

Dear Colleagues;

Writing articles about, contributing to discussions on, or just earnestly discussing in foyers this subject of the relationship between 'mainstream' and 'experimental' theatre/performance practice is something that I seem to have been doing fairly solidly since 1982, which is when I first started making what I have always stubbornly called *shows*, and what other people have variously called theatre, experimental theatre, fringe theatre, gay theatre, site-specific theatre, performance art, live art, drag, music theatre, chamber opera, oratorio and even *plays* – depending on where and when they were being performed, and who was watching them and why. However, here we go again...

For the purposes of this letter, I am going to try and give a concise account of some specific, and, I hope salient, ambitions and tactics that were part of a very particular large-scale and long-term project: my work as Artistic Director of the Lyric Hammersmith, a job which I did from 1994 to 2004 in symbiotic partnership with Simon Mellor, who was Executive Director/Producer of the building for that entire period, and without whom nothing much would have happened.

Any orderliness in my account will of course be largely spurious; anyone who downplays the roles of both luck and financial pressure in the achievements of any artistic enterprise – and particularly a building-based one – is more or less lying. Everything that our work at the Lyric did, and didn't, achieve was done under constant and almost-crippling financial pressure, and in the context of the extremely and increasingly competitive and crowded world of London theatre.

Before I start to describe some of the things which Simon and I thought and did about this consistently vexed question of the mainstream and the experimental, here are a few points to try and indicate where we were coming from in 1994:

1. Back in 1982, there had been a pretty absolute set of divisions between plays and formally innovative work; between building-based 'theatre' and project-funded touring/arts centre/small-scale 'experimental theatre'; between 'political' work and work which sought to 'entertain.' By 1994, these divisions, it seemed to us, were in meltdown. We were not prepared to be boxed up any longer. This was mostly because…

2. By 1994, I had already tested these divisions to the limit as an artist – I had worked in contexts and venues ranging from the National Theatre and Royal Court at one end (doing a classic eighteenth century comedy in the former and a radical queer performance musical comedy in the latter) to the National Review of Live Art, the Institute of Contemporary Arts (ICA), derelict warehouses, the Drill Hall, Southwark Cathedral and gay clubs at the other (doing drag, queer devised performance, chamber opera, large scale experimental music theatre … categories fail me). In between, I had played just about every arts centre that hosted small scale touring experimental work in the country. This had been done via the company I was part of, GLORIA.

3. As a gay artist who had started in the 1980s and flowered in the 1990s, I had a very particular take on the division between high and low art, between mainstream and experimental, between popular and precious – the division that dogs every corner of the British creative establishment, and that I personally loathe; to put it simply, I was part of a culture in which such divisions were patently nonsense. Michael Clark, Fassbinder, Derek Jarman, Frankie Goes to Hollywood, the radical 'powerhouse' regime at the London Coliseum and the glorious, glorious work of the Glasgow Citizens, Philip Hedley's work as producer at Theatre Royal Stratford East – to name but a few of my heroes back in the early days – all made it clear that the journalistic and Arts Council

categories of what was formally or politically radical, what was popular, what was 'big' and what was 'small' or 'minor' or 'fringe' were all a bit hidebound and unambitious.

4. If you tour for long enough, you get very tired of re-inventing the wheel, of constantly re-negotiating relationships with the performance space, with the technical crew, with the marketing department, with performers, and there are precious few opportunities to build up skills or momentum. And you are always having to constantly renegotiate your funding deals. Most importantly, you have little chance to build up a relationship with an audience, of which more later.

Within those contexts, here are some of the key ways we tried to put our various grievances and ambitions into practice:

1. We dared to assume that the architecture and traditions of the proscenium playhouse – two words that were absolute anathema to most self-appointed radicals in 1994 – might themselves be radical and pleasurable in equal measure. Or, to put it another way, that this might be a site it was worth being specific about. We proposed that having an ambition to play to 500 people night after night for weeks on end (something that in practice we very, very rarely achieved) might be a wonderful thing. That colour, extravagance, theatricality and live music in a night out might be fantastic. That the active, dynamic, intimate, relationship between the performer and the audience presupposed by the architecture of a great playhouse like the Lyric might be something that one should (as manager and producer as well as an artist) try and inculcate in a new generation of young performers, devisers and directors. That the red-velvet-and-gilded-plasterwork cliché might actually be an environment specifically well-suited to inspiring and provoking and supporting transgressive work (if that sounds abstract, then I would quote my own extremist productions of the politically radical costume dramas of Maugham, Rattigan and Genet, not to mention the even kinkier pleasures of rare Marivaux, Kleist and late Shakespeare; the deliriously dotty ideas of inviting Improbable to devise a pantomime or Frantic Assembly or

Tamasha to essay actual musicals (physical theatre and music-theatre, they liked to call it – we didn't mind, so long as it was a musical); of inviting Kneehigh to get down and dirty with classic adaptation or Victoria Chaplin to make a kids show). Too often, in our experience, the 'experimental' has been dogged by a nasty taste of Puritanism – by the supposed 'seriousness' and implicit superiority of either new writing or 'performance' and their black-box studio settings – and we were having none of that.

2.   There was an unspoken assumption in the late 1980s and early 1990s that 'large scale' radical work could only be produced on a site-specific basis, or in the context of a festival, or with the protection of an international profile/reputation. While some of these tactics – ones which I had employed myself – were great as stepping stones, it seemed to me very important that the aesthetic and practical, production-skill lessons learnt from the big one-offs were then re-invested in a more continuous, accessible practice. Otherwise, there was a real danger that new British work would retreat into an upward spiral of two-nights-only one-off extravaganzas – high-profile, high-cost, high-class, high-hype but not really providing any working model for change and growth for audiences or performers or funding bodies or venue-based producers.

3.   Without telling anyone we were doing it, we responded to the very particular environment of an Edwardian playhouse by foregrounding the visually and physically adventurous – even (especially) when we were doing ostensibly 'literary' plays. This is where we put into practice the lessons we had learnt from all that 1980's so-called 'visual theatre' stuff – Bausch, Lepage, Wooster Group, all the companies who were our peers at the ICA. We achieved this by consistently working with artists of the calibre of (for instance) Rae Smith, Ian McNeil, Robin Whitmore, Paule Constable and Rick Fisher. This meant that over a period of years we were able to gradually erode at the most basic level of what people were actually watching the public perception that plays, literary adaptations, Christmas shows and kids shows were somehow ranked against devised work, physical work and

'multicultural' work in an oppositional hierarchy of theatrical radical-ness versus traditional-ness. Whatever the show, it was never old-fashioned, because it was produced to the highest possible standards by radically-minded designers. The old chestnut about visual/physical = radical vs. literary = old-fashioned/boring was gradually eroded. Please note that this took years, was a bloody struggle, and caused great trouble at the box office as audiences and critics and fellow-practitioners have very fixed minds on these matters. They like things in tidy categories. They want to be told what is experimental and what is not.

4. We worked on the assumption that radical work had rights of possession over the main house. Too often, in our touring experience during the 1980s, the studio space attached to a main house was really a guilt-absolving space, where the 'radical' was kept in its place, with small audiences and production budgets; there was no bridge between the two spaces. Therefore, whenever budget constraints allowed, we would identify and hunt down companies who we could put in the studio specifically in order to initiate a long-term relationship; to introduce a company to the larger culture of the building, the problems and ambitions of larger scale work; to share skills in production and marketing; to start to build an audience which they could eventually take upstairs with them; to begin to talk to them about how their work would have to grow and develop if it was to move upstairs. This last point is very important; in order for Improbable, Frantic Assembly, Kneehigh, Tamasha and The Right Size and others to make main-house shows, they had to be seduced and inspired into doing that – the work itself has to grow, it can't just be transplanted.

5. We actively sought out places where performers from one tradition could cross over into another. When then-performance-artist Emily Woof proposed a large-scale piece dealing with sexuality, to access an audience of teenage girls, we worked with her on a new staging of *Romeo and Juliet*. We seduced large and various audiences into watching determinedly radical stagings of

feminist/queer dramas by casting Joanna Lumley, Sheila Hancock, Maggie Steed, Anita Dobson, Jack Davenport and Julian Clary in them. We smuggled radical non-theatre artistes Neil Tennant, the Ridiculous Theatre's Everett Quinton, Gary Carter, Guy Dartnell, Bette Bourne and Julian Bleach into (respectively) Wilde, Genet, Marivaux, Shakespeare, and a one-night special with Alan Rickman and the Brodsky Quartet. We got people who would never dream of sitting in a proper theatre to come and see The Magnetic Fields, Victoria Chaplin, and The Tiger Lilies – and discover that they were in a great and groovy place. For audiences and artists alike, we actively sought to create a building culture which proposed points of collision and collusion between the 'theatre' and new traditions of performance, rather than division.

6. (And this last point is the Only Thing I Really Care About). The only important difference between 'theatre' and 'experimental theatre/performance', as far as I'm concerned, is that the former takes its audience as a given, whereas the latter is always seeking to extend and challenge and deepen its relationship with the audience, both formally and – most importantly – socially. To put it at its bluntest, main-house theatre looks to the pre-existent audience of the past, new theatre to the audience of the future. Our bright ideas in this department were;

   a) All first night performances were free to anyone who lived and worked in the borough. This meant that no-one could say that the work wasn't 'for them' – it announced in one stroke that we thought Robert Lepage and Tamasha and Kleist and Cinderella staged by Improbable were all equally worthy of their interest (this idea was nicked from the Glasgow's Citizens' Theatre). It meant that the most surprising people got to see the most surprising things. It sent out a very clear message.

   b) We made a lot of noise about there always being one night a week when tickets were dirt cheap, encouraging the idea of experiment and loyalty. Opening doors, not announcing exclusivity…. This idea has since become very popular elsewhere.

c) We put an enormous amount of effort into creating a culture within the building, and then outside the building – in marketing, in press, in the house style, which expressed a determined radicalism and catholicity of taste – no snobbism about (and this is crucial) EITHER the experimental or the mainstream – an abolition of those categories, in effect. I would say this was multiculturalism in its widest sense. Getting audiences used to the idea that they might be sitting next to people NOT like them. (Again, this is a big one as audiences – radical and traditional alike – really don't like things getting too mixed up, specifically class- or age-wise).

d) We put a huge amount of money and effort into our education programme, making it absolutely central to the work and public life of the building, not some guilty or apologetic socially responsible add-on. We realised very early on that it is often artists perceived as 'radical' or 'experimental' who are best placed to create work for younger audiences, and to encourage them to own the building and its shows.

e) At all times and in all places, on every opening night, we asked ourselves this question: WHO IS THIS FOR? WHO IS COMING UP OUR STAIRS?

It was a blast. Perhaps it is as simple as thinking of a theatre-building as a fantastic place, not a problem to be solved.

Yours sincerely,

Neil Bartlett.

Neil Bartlett is a director and author. His early work was as a performance artist; from 1994-2004 he was Artistic Director of the Lyric Hammersmith. Along the way, he has created work for venues and institutions as various as the ICA, the Drill Hall, the National Review of Live Art, the National Theatre, Artangel, the Royal Court, Battersea Arts Centre, the Derby Playhouse, the American Repertory Theatre, the Royal Shakespeare Company, several derelict warehouses, almost every arts centre in the country, Southwark Cathedral and the Vauxhall Tavern.
www.neil-bartlett.com

Whistling

Stella Hall

in the Dark

Why is it that they say of live theatre that one bad experience can put some overly sensitive audience members off for life? In other artforms a woeful gig or yet another Hollywood flop can still see them bouncing back for more. Why don't they take the risk and go back into that darkened room where live performers wait?

I've seen my fair share of indifferent work over the years and there is at least one theatre the pattern of whose upholstery I could, to this day, draw for you blindfold. I sat in agony throughout Peter Brook's *The Ik,* praying for a divine intervention either to make me see what others saw, or to take me away from this corporeal existence. But, with boundless optimism, I still enter those doors each time in hope of transportation of a different kind. Since being taken as a teen to London to see Le Grand Magic Circus at the Roundhouse and Andy Warhol's Marilyns and Campbell's Soup Cans, I have looked for artists who will transport me, out of the here and now, into their world.

I do not believe I am unusual in that, and with a normal human desire for company, I seek to develop audiences who are looking for the same thing. I've worked professionally in that longed-for world over the last twenty odd years in at least seven of our major UK cities, attempting to put together coherent programmes in arts centres and festivals in each, trying to connect with the very different audiences in these different places. I have found audiences in Manchester behave differently from those in Coventry, London, Belfast and now NewcastleGateshead. Touring artists already know these fine tunings; as audiences we laugh at different things, cough at different moments, remain obstinately silent when a response is anticipated – gasp in the 'wrong' places.

As Peter Sellars once told delegates at the *Urban Hymns* symposium in Nottingham, '..you have to figure out what an audience wants… and figure out a way to give it to them.' That figuring out takes time. Presenters have to get to know their audience, to feel their pulse, see what works and what doesn't work. That's hellish for the festival director who only gets one go a year, and not so great either for the programmer who needs to roll up her sleeves and go as soon as she arrives at her desk.

In the beginning though, before any 'getting to know you', it's about jumping into that unknown pool and taking the risk, hoping you've got it nearly right and hoping the audience will risk with you. In the past I have lectured on programming and run courses for programmers for the Independent Theatre Council (ITC) with marketeers talking about the marketing mix; rising stars, cash cows, dead dogs (though I've never believed in dead dogs) … There really is an audience for every performance, you just have to find it, and be truthful while you are at it. I don't believe in easy work and I don't believe in easy answers, but an audience mustn't be deceived or they will never return, and no artist will thank you for misrepresentation. Don't pretend hip hop dancers performing to the occasional tinkling of Tibetan bells is accessible performance for all the family – it isn't. Nor is Karen Finley covering herself in egg yolks and feathers immediately available to any viewer (but those who saw her in The Green Room's opening season knew what they were in for and remember it with as much pride as that select few at the Sex Pistols' first gig). For a presenter, there is nothing as satisfying as seeing that invisible bond between an audience who have come through a challenging show together.

If it doesn't work and they don't even turn up (a risk that is built into every programming decision) you can console yourself by saying it was an idea before its time. In my first year at the Belfast Festival I sat with 40 people in a 300 seat auditorium watching Victoria from Ghent present their miraculous production of *Ubung*. Performers aged twelve to sixteen voiced their badly-behaving adult counterparts on a silent film projected onto a downstage screen. It spoke movingly and with the lightest touch of how we adults influence a child's development. I now realise it was too early to present that show; we had not grown the audience for it. Two years later, after a major audience development programme, we could have filled those seats, but I still believe it was a risk worth taking.

Freudian psychoanalysts at the turn of the twentieth century concluded it was not normal to overcome natural fears at all, and that risk-taking behaviour was evidence of a diseased mind. Fortunately for us twenty-first centurions that is no longer widely held to be true! Contemporary thinkers say that although some people are undoubtedly 'riskier' than others, we have evolved as a species to take risks in order to survive. Certainly I don't believe programmers can survive without risk, and with risk comes the possibility of failure. We need long range goals to keep us from short range failures and for me, that goal is all about finding ways to introduce beautiful and challenging work to audiences, and finding partners in passion with whom to do it.

In 1983 Jeremy Shine and I co-founded The Green Room in Manchester. It was the first multi-artform venue in the city and funds had been set aside by the departing Greater Manchester Council for its establishment. The owners of the first venue we chose – an amateur dramatic club – mislaid the title deeds and we were forced into a wandering life, promoting events in a host of different places. Happily, it was the basis for a philosophy of partnership that hasn't changed since.

We worked together with all the venues in the city, matching artists to locations. Trickster flew from the steel tubing of the Royal Exchange, we presented the Institute of Contemporary Arts' (ICA) *Performing Clothes* with Leigh Bowery at the Hacienda, Impact Theatre strutted their beautiful stuff in *The Carrier Frequency* at the Royal Northern College of Music and we heaved Lumiere and Son's sets down the steep steps to the Library Theatre stage. In Didsbury, drama students walked out after a day's rehearsal as we got shows in. I wanted to grab them by the hair and yank them back, saying 'look what you're missing!' But they were going on to be different kinds of theatre makers, or television actors, and didn't connect with what we thought to be some of the finest artists of our age; Hesitate and Demonstrate, Forkbeard Fantasy, IOU (who I really believed had dug down to another realm below the stage), People Show, Station House Opera – some introduced by Artsadmin, a key partner over the years, some identified directly. We staged Forced Entertainment's second show, *Nighthawks* in 1985 in the basement of the Adult Education Centre on Oxford Road, the beginning of a long and fruitful relationship which would go on to the commissioning of *Dreams Winter* a site specific work for Central Library. LIFT began life in 1981 and in 1983 we jointly programmed MIFT (an unfortunate acronym!) beginning a partnership which saw international work regularly visiting the city over the years.

Finally in 1989 we opened our own venue under the railway arches in Whitworth Street, sleeping there on the nights before opening since the alarms weren't working and frankly we couldn't bear to be away. Home at last to all those touring companies who had slummed it in Birch Community Centre or the Brickhouse, Contact's very basic studio, and home to the countless artists growing up in Manchester; Doo Cot, Whalley Range Allstars, New Breed, The Glee Club, Rivca Rubin and Michael Mayhew. All of these made it a place of shared ideas and experiment.

New companies and artists emerged from the old; Steve Shill, Graeme Miller, Heather Ackroyd, Alison Andrews. And work from Gary Stevens, Bobby Baker, Dogs in Honey, Gay Sweatshop, Improbable, motiroti, desperate optimists and DV8 were part of the roll call. So were Women's Theatre Group, Them Wifies, Mrs Worthington's Daughters, and Black Theatre Co-operative. The Green Room was part of a national circuit, with Neil Wallace and Janek Alexander at Chapter in Cardiff; Michael Morris then Lois Keidan and Catherine Ugwu at the ICA; Nikki Milican at Midland Group, Nottingham, then the Third Eye Centre; and a small group of others who kept each other informed and buoyed up when it began to seem like a huge burden to be running a building, when so much exciting work was happening well outside traditional boundaries.

But what was this? The world music audiences, which had been so plentiful at the Royal Northern College of Music (RNCM), didn't want to come in such numbers to The Green Room, and narrative theatre work, so successful when presented by us in the Library Theatre, didn't fare as well either. What next? The producing theatres would be programming the work themselves, taking bread from the mouths of honest arts centres! And they did. The audiences behaved differently in different venues too, and that's not just because they were a different group of people – there was obviously an overlap, but because the context had changed and the new location shaped the perception of an audience as to its relative merits and value. So, work presented in a funky railway arch had its context shaped for it in the same way as work presented in the hallowed surroundings of the Royal Exchange, the region's premier theatre.

Despite our much vaunted commitment to partnership, it was at first another matter when what we saw as our role was being usurped. We really thought the reps should stick to producing plays and let us do the rest. It seems foolish now; the world has changed and few theatres can afford, or desire, to produce year round. But such was the sense of separation at the time that few theatres chose to invite experimental touring work in for other than financial reasons. It certainly wasn't initially a passion for the work.

However, there were exceptions, and these grew, year on year. People like Neil Bartlett took on the Lyric Hammersmith, Ruth Mackenzie went to Nottingham Playhouse. A new generation of theatre-makers were introducing diversity in a way that has changed the face of our building based companies ever since.

Meanwhile, Stephen Daldry invited me in to run the annual Barclays New Stages Festival at the Royal Court Theatre. This scheme provided new funds to make experimental work and was a truly welcome addition to the limited support available through the Arts Council. For several years I worked with an impressive marketing team who cross-sold Rose English, Stan's Café, NVA, Ralf Ralf, Semblance, Forced Entertainment and a host of others to audiences who thought that what they really wanted was the English Stage Company and new writing but decided that they would take a little risk. Who cared if the Royal Court's initial motivation was financial and that Barclays paid for us to present work during the difficult summer months? We were able to commission Pete Brooks with the Islington Festival and Bobby Baker with the Chelsea Physic Garden. It was an arranged marriage with benefits to all. The programme raised the profile of artists who would never have appeared in those surroundings otherwise. CandoCo were the first disabled artists to appear on that stage, and motiroti the first Asian company. The partnership with LIFT continued and a new one, with Pride, began. We co-presented Edward Lam and the Handsome Foundation, helping the Royal Court build new audiences for their commission to Lloyd Newson of DV8.

Sadly, not all experiments work out. Barclays took advice from others with different agendas and, despite protests, decided to put their funds into slightly less challenging middle scale touring work. One or two of the companies had in fact been unsuited to that confining stage, and unhappy with the attitudes to artists from a fine art or live art background of some technicians steeped in West End practices. Negative, unwelcoming, some practised a level of separatism that exemplified all that was worst in what Barry Rutter often described as 'velvet theatre'. Some, but by no means all. Bad old habits die hard, and no doubt they are still on display in the deepest reaches of theatres where one dare not mention Macbeth, nor whistle.

Thankfully, these attitudes were not in evidence at Warwick Arts Centre where I joined a devoted team including the current director Alan Rivett to deliver a huge range of events. Here, the great pleasure of working with a curator of the skill and knowledge of Sarah Shalgosky enabled real linkages between performance, live art and the visual arts to be made. Lois Keidan assisted on developing a fledgling live art programme which I am proud to say still continues thanks to partnerships with Mark Ball of Fierce.

There were different challenges in Northern Ireland. An earlier Festival Director had described the Belfast Festival at Queen's as 'neutral', and indeed to be successful, many events there must take place in neutral locations. But art is anything but neutral; it must engage, and I therefore set out to find an active engagement with a range of cultural communities. It didn't work with *Ubung,* but in partnership with the Ormeau Baths Gallery, the Old Museum, and the Lyric Theatre – all looking to build new relationships with audiences – many new experiences happened. Quarantine guided blindfolded audiences through *Something a Taxi Driver in Liverpool Said*, Improbable brought *Sticky* to 7,000 people from all backgrounds and Pure Movement connected young people from both sides of the divide. However, mistakes continued: In 2001, I was naively unprepared for sectarianism to flare up at the invitation to a young Israeli dance troupe to perform. Petitions against it were written, signed by local artists participating in the Festival, and demonstrations took place outside the venue as audiences ran the gauntlet of photographers from the Andersonstown News. Several members of the Nationalist community made political capital out of the visit which we refused to cancel, unwilling to penalise artists for the views of the government under which they laboured. It was a difficult time, and demonstrated only too clearly the need to wait and listen, get to know a place and figure out what the audiences there really need.

I'm now in a place where yet another generation are doing the figuring out, and getting better at it all the time. Erica Whyman at Northern Stage is inviting artists to process into her new building and construct castles in the air outside it, and John McGrath at Contact Theatre is bringing in an audience who once would simply have kicked a ball against the outside wall.

Edison did sixteen hundred experiments before he invented the light bulb. When a friend asked why he was wasting so much time and not achieving anything he answered that of course he'd accomplished something – he'd learnt 1,600 ways it doesn't work! Over the years I must have made at least sixteen hundred mistakes but one has to keep moving forward. Fear is false expectations appearing real and fear of failure can be a paralyzing thing. It can make us take the easy route, or not even go on the journey. But, as Peter Sellars wrote, 'probably some of the most awesome and beautiful and powerful things we can do will fail.'

Stella Hall is Creative Director of the Newcastle Gateshead Initative. Previously she was Director of the Belfast Festival at Queens and Director of Warwick Arts Centre. She played a key role in Manchester's successful bid to be the 1994 City of Drama, was the Royal Court Theatre's Barclay's New Stages Festival Director, and was the Founding Artistic Director of Green Room Arts Centre in Manchester.

Working with Ra-Ra Zoo,
Archaos and Bow Gamelan in
the 1980's was my first taste
of how the experimental can
inform the mainstream. Their
disregard for convention and
ability to work at established
venues was a huge influence
on my work today and Crying
Out Loud continues this ethos
by working with artists at mid
scale venues, James Thiérrée
being the best example. "My
idea of education is to unsettle
the minds of the young and
inflame their intellects"
(Robert Maynard Hutchins) is
COLs current moto.
Rachel Clare, Director,
Crying Out Loud

As Natural as Breathing
John E McGrath

A few months ago I had the opportunity to see a work in progress by a talented emerging artist who had first become involved in Contact as a participant in our young people's programmes over six years ago. This young artist had made a solo show about the relationship between a young black man in Manchester and his Jamaican father, and the performance was a moving and sometimes disturbing portrayal of life in today's Britain. Watching the show, though, what impressed me wasn't just the raw, honest subject matter, but the confident, experimental form in which it was presented. Without needing to flash any deconstructive angst around, the performance integrated an impressive and thoughtful range of approaches to theatre into an edgy, self-aware whole

Afterwards I had a chat with the young theatre-maker who had created the piece, and admitted to him that while I'd been expecting to be impressed by his work – as I knew how talented he was – I'd been surprised at his confidence in experimenting with form. He laughed and told me that he'd learned a lot in all of the workshops he'd done at Contact, but that probably one of the most transformative things he'd done with us was take a job as an usher. While earning five pounds an hour each night for two years, he'd sat in the theatre watching everyone from Forced Entertainment to Benji Reid, from Quarantine to The Builders Association and motiroti. When he came to make his own work, he found all of these theatrical languages pumping through his blood. Experiment was as natural to him as breathing.

Contact is a theatre space dedicated to new performance and to young people. With participation at the core of everything we do, and a 'ninety nine per cent new work on stage' policy, we have developed a theatre-making environment that differs radically from the models both of regional producing theatre and of the presenting arts centre. Every day at Contact, new work is being made. Sometimes this is a play with a writer and a director and a cast of Equity actors, sometimes it is a group of emerging artists in a residency together. Sometimes it is ambitious new work with young people, often working alongside some of the most exciting contemporary practitioners, from Belgium's Victoria to Manchester's Quarantine. But because this daily business of making work is done in such a variety of ways, its outcomes can also be very various. There will be weeks when every space in the building – from theatres, to rehearsal room, to foyers – are all filled with artists showing new work they have made in the building. Other times a whole month may go by with only one or two performances of work that has developed inside Contact.

With a wide-ranging programme of workshops and residencies always in full swing, it would be quite possible to run Contact as a space that opened its doors to an audience only on the occasions when we had created a new piece of work. We would certainly still have plenty to keep us busy. And in some ways this would seem to fit our core focus of new performance and young people. However, there is a whole other aspect to what we do, which sits alongside these developmental activities, and informs them in a vital way: our programme of visiting work.

As well as the work that we produce with artists and young people in the building, Contact presents a busy programme of new work from visiting companies. Some of these companies have a long relationship with us, and have become partners with whom we collaborate on a regular basis. Others may simply be artists who we feel are doing something exciting, and whose work we would like to share with our audiences. The programme includes work by a huge range of companies. Many of them produce 'experimental theatre'.

We see the artists and companies who visit us as intrinsic to the creative life of our theatre. We try to provide as welcoming and as social a space as possible, not just because we want to be nice, but because we hope that these visiting artists will relax enough to spend time with the artists and young people around and about the building. We want them to leave ideas, opinions and techniques behind, to leave us changed in some way.

Of course, workshop programmes, outreach projects, audience development initiatives can all be part of this work, and with our audience primarily under 35 years old, we are competing with a lot of other attractions to gain their attention and loyalty. But all the marketing initiatives in the world can't begin to approach the effect of a young performer from Lonsight, Rusholme, Moss Side, or Moston accidentally ending up in a discussion with an experimental performance artist from Holland or New York, as both wait for the kettle in the green room to boil, or as they find themselves sharing the same table in the bar.

To separate 'experimental theatre' out as needing different study or skills – something that both the education system and the funding bodies are often keen to do – is to forget that for artists, and for young people, experiment should be as natural as breathing. While a substantial conservative theatre audience may well want its drama served in recognisably 'well-made' dish at a realistically-rendered, period-appropriate dining table, or delivered by a well-spoken ensemble of attractive RADA-trained all-rounders; for the majority of the population all theatre is an experiment, a leap of faith, a rarity.

At Contact, the single programming choice that most strikes fear into our marketing staff is a piece of well-made drama. This isn't to say that we don't take the risk, and when a company, such as Paines Plough, has a reputation for consistently high-quality, provocative work, the audiences will come, and come back. But in general for our young audiences, the biggest fear is that theatre will be boring. Forced Entertainment, Quarantine, Company F.Z, motiroti, may be challenging, strange, difficult and sometimes even annoying, but they are very rarely dull. And so we can programme them with confidence, and people will come: young people, from a range of backgrounds, for a range of reasons. Some of them will walk out before the end. Others will come back next time and bring their friends.

A successful theatre director once complimented me on the niche we had built at Contact. It was meant as a compliment, but I took it as a challenge. 'We don't have a niche', I replied. 'You have the niche. In the so-called mainstream houses, with their subscriber audiences, the same few thousand people turning up again and again. That's the niche. We have everyone else!'

Of course, I was lying. We have a good number of people coming to Contact, and many of them go away with a fair bit of theatrical experiment in their blood. But there's a whole lot more people still to reach. What I am absolutely convinced of is that they will never be reached by the kind of theatre that is habitually described as mainstream. Commercial theatre may find a lot of them: good spectacle will always have a role. But the kind of stodge that is served up as well made theatre in subsidised venues will only ever play to a minority crowd.

The dichotomy between experimental and mainstream benefits no-one, it marginalises one side and fossilises the other. Good theatre is always an experiment. And the way to find audiences is to invite them, in an enjoyable way, to share in the experiment.

So, at Contact, we attempt to create an open, exploratory environment, which is as accessible and engaging to a sixteen year old from Cheetham Hill as it is to a fifty year old performance art legend from New York City. And by and large it works. Figures such as New York's Penny Arcade return to Contact with glee because they can meet people they would never meet in more rarefied experimental environments. And any artist worth their salt knows that running into the same bunch of people on the same international or national circuit can never be good for the creative soul.

We avoid, where possible, over-categorising work. We don't have a main house or a studio programme – when you book a show, we don't tell you what space it is in until you arrive. We try to avoid over-segmenting our marketing. Yes we may send you a flier for The Builders Association if you came to the recent Forced Entertainment show, but we may send you information on Benji Reid, or a new club night, or the artist residency programme too.

We don't have a subscriber audience. We battle for every audience member for every show. Sometimes our efforts may work better than others, but we are never stuck with trying to fulfil the expectations of a single core group.

We involve our audience in our programming. Through our Action Contact project, audience members can become involved in developing the programme, going out to see work, feeding back on proposals for shows, and evaluating the work we put on. A feisty, committed group of young programmers regularly surprises me with their tastes, and often guesses the audience response better than I do.

Just as we put participation at the heart of everything we do, so we encourage experiment at all levels. Our workshop programmes are all developed as artistic experiments, trying out something new. We train artists from a truly diverse range of backgrounds – in terms of artform, culture and experience – to develop work with young people. And we support them properly. Many artists, particularly with experimental companies, have had bad experiences in the past on poorly managed projects, often being asked to work alone, or with inappropriate groups. We try to match artists and young people in a thoughtful if challenging way. We want both sides to come out wanting to do this again!

We ask workshop artists to work in new teams, to surprise and learn from each other, at the same time as challenging participants.

We provide a wide range of 'emerging artist' programmes, where participants can start to define themselves as artists, where young artists can come and work with us for the first time, and where more established artist can change gear or try something new. We set these up in structures where interaction and shared learning will be at the heart of things.

Like all experimenters, sometimes we fail. There have been shows that next to no-one has come to. There have been participatory projects that have seemed radical, but have produced predictable, unexciting work. There have been residencies that have been unsatisfying or unhappy. When these things happen, we try to learn something, because the only bad experiment is one that teaches you nothing.

And sometimes we succeed gloriously. Such as the time we won an award and decided that the prize money should be spent on asking two artists who had never worked together to make an experimental theatre piece with any young people from Contact they wanted to choose. The only rule was that the show should be called *Manchester*. I'd expected something unusual, but probably full of Manchester energy: the music, the clubs, the street style. The mysterious, meditative installation that Juliet Ellis and Craig Conway developed with six of Contact's young people (a couple of whom had, just a few years ago, been among the most 'challenging' of our participants) was wonderfully, disturbingly, like nothing I had imagined. These young performers had developed a style of performance so subtle, suggestive and strange, that you felt like you were being taken into a world where the rules existed only for this moment, and only in their hands. Experiment had become as natural to them as breathing.

So, I suspect that experimental theatre will thrive most in our venues when we accept that all theatre must be an experiment, and that there can be accessible, funny, engaging experiments, just as there can be challenging, difficult, disturbing experiments. When we stop trying to explain experiment to audiences and instead listen to them explaining their reactions to us. When we market each show on its unique characteristics, and not on some judgement as to who ought to like it. When we stop trying to amuse the same few people every week, and go out and find some new people. When we allow experimental artists to inhabit venues, not just visit them on sufferance now and then. And when we embrace the many young theatre artists for whom experiment is a natural, enjoyable, everyday way of looking at the world.

John E McGrath is Artistic Director of Contact Manchester. As a director, recent collaborations have been with Lemn Sissay, Kaite O'Reilly, Paul Clay, Benji Reid and Penny Arcade. He is the author of *Loving Big Brother: Performance, Privacy and Surveillance Space* (Routledge), and was recently awarded a NESTA Cultural Leadership Award.
www.contact-theatre.org

I can recommend the ride!

Alan Rivett

I remember the moment well. It was as if a coming of age ritual. Nothing was said, just a look – to share and to read on another's face. Standing at the back of Warwick Arts Centre's steeply raked 550 seat theatre with Tim Etchells of Forced Entertainment, ready for the start of a performance of *First Night* in October 2001 with a full house extending all around us. This was the culmination of many years of hard work by a lot of people making new work and the shared look was the summing up, neither triumphant nor overindulgent, more of a realisation that this was probably quite an important moment for both of us. The fact was that after twenty year of passion for experimental work, squeezed into studio spaces, not being able to programme everything every time, losing productions to Europe, taking on doubt, guilt, moving on from difficult conversations without resolution; here we were with a full main house for a Forced Entertainment show!

But where had we come from to arrive here? I'm sure part of the answer lies in the idea of an 'Arts Centre'; a place where mainstream and experiment can cohabit and, in the minds of many, should cohabit. I have been inclined to reject the idea of the 'mainstream' as dominant cultures always evolve. I well remember the moment when radical left wing theatre company Belt and Braces arrived in the West End with Dario Fo's *Accidental Death of an Anarchist*. For those of us working in community theatre at the time this was not just a confirmation that the mainstream was evolving but an affirmation that what we were engaged in, experiment with form and content, would inherit the mainstream! So let's not be prescriptive in our descriptions and categorisation (leave this to the bureaucrats).

Warwick Arts Centre, since opening in 1974 has maintained a programme of work by experimental artists. This has waxed and waned over the last thirty years depending on the interests of the Arts Centre Director and the nature of work being made. Artists and companies such as IOU, Bobby Baker, Stationhouse Opera and Forced Entertainment had an established (though erratic) part of Warwick Arts Centre's programme during the 1990s. The experimental / live art programme was given a significant lift on the arrival of Stella Hall as Director in 1998. Stella, a lifetime champion of experimental work, nurtured from her founding of Manchester's Green Room, put this strand of programming firmly into the organisation's consciousness. Serious collaboration with the Fierce Festival, consistency of programming, linking to UK and international live art networks and talking to live and experimental artists became the norm. The list of artists and companies playing to sizeable audiences grew: Goat Island, Franko B, Ron Athey, Gob Squad, Ursula Martinez, Marisa Carnesky and Kazuko Hohki all took their part in the programme, most, more than once and will continue to do so. Why? Because (and this is surely up for debate) as a multi disciplinary arts centre I believe we have a responsibility to artists to nurture their work and provide a platform for it.

What about audiences? We have a responsibility to them too, but if audiences' interest in experimental work is negligible then it's really not worthwhile either for the organisation or the artists. Finding and encouraging audiences to experience experimental work thus becomes part of our job. This isn't so different to other parts of Warwick Arts Centre's programme. We work at exposing classical music audiences to Bruckner, Messaian, Bertwhistle and Adams; so what's the difference in approach in introducing audiences to Station House Opera and Gob Squad? Well, context is everything. Warwick Arts Centre exists in a university where students study performance; it exists in the West Midlands with a population of over three million people; with Fierce an annual festival of experimental performance; there are University and FE lecturers leading their students to an appreciation of experimental performance; and the practice of companies such as Forced Entertainment and DV8 are included for study on Post-16 exam course curricula. Though a minority interest, it is clear that sufficient enthusiasm exists for experimental work to attract audiences alongside the mainstream. There is a twin track approach which goes some way to securing the successful outcome of a well-attended performance for experimental work:

1. consistency of programming
2. knowing and tracking 'champions' among the potential audience.

Simply slotting an appearance by a live or experimental artist or company into a season and them forgetting about this programme for another year will lead to tears. Audiences need to know that the organisation is serious about experimental work to give it a coherent and consistent presence. Artists also need the assurance that they are not always being asked to be 'trailblazers' with nothing to follow.

'Champions', teachers, lecturers, other artists (to name a few) need nurturing, forward notice, to be listened to and taken notice of. They are the conduits to larger numbers of like-minded people who will, if treated well, bring other audiences with them.

Let's not be over optimistic though. Consistency and care for champions takes time and will. These are so easily over-ridden by any number of pressing issues which arise in most venues most of the time: financial imperatives, reluctance to take too many risks with the programme, and political interference.

All the above accepted, experimental work continues to be largely locked into studio sized dimensions in both gallery and performance space. The exception is grand site specific work, largely too expensive and complex for a venue to take on.

Our case study of Marisa Carnesky's *Ghost Train* and the Clod Ensemble's *Red Ladies* suggests that nothing is impossible given strong powers of persuasion and enduring partnerships (as well as a healthy dose of bloodymindedness).

There are three specific contributing factors to the success of these extraordinary events:

1. a time specific/political need for Warwick Arts Centre to reposition itself in relation to Coventry as a city, it's citizens and the political decision makers
2. Coventry, as a location in the West Midlands sharing in a major way in the region wide Fierce Festival
3. the ability to form real partnerships to assist delivery.

Fierce and Warwick Arts Centre had maintained a well-articulated interest in Marisa Carnesky's *Ghost Train* since hearing the initial idea. This matured fairly quickly into a joint financial contribution as co-commissioners. At the same time a separate and specific campaign was underway to convince opinion formers in Coventry that Warwick Arts Centre was a 'part of the City's cultural infrastructure' to counter arguments that as an 'out of town university based facility', Warwick Arts Centre had little relevance to the people of Coventry. *Ghost Train* was the perfect vehicle to demonstrate in a palpable way that Warwick Arts Centre and Fierce Festival had a genuine place in Coventry and for Coventry people all that was needed was a partnership to assist in the delivery of a complex and intricate project. CV One, Coventry's unique and skilled city centre management company were the perfect partners. CV One provided all on site logistical support, utilities, equipment hire services and licensing. Warwick Arts Centre maintained overall project management responsibility with Fierce Festival providing all 'front of house' on site personnel. *Ghost Train*, which had had a somewhat chequered life up to the point of arrival in Coventry in May 2005, operated like a dream for a week during *Fierce '05*. It performed to 100% audience capacity, developed creatively under Marisa's guidance during its visit to Coventry and received very positive audience feedback.

The Red Ladies project, under the creative direction of the Clod Ensemble has just happened in Coventry. Drawing on the *Ghost Train* experience our objective was to secure partners in Coventry, perform the work entirely in Coventry to a Coventry and Fierce audience. It didn't work as planned! City centre space became unavailable, logistical support for the kind of event envisaged was seen as uncertain and the decision was made to revert to a daily Red Ladies mission in the city centre and an evening performance (involving 22 Red Ladies!) at Warwick Arts Centre. Again, in collaboration with *Fierce '06*, the Red Ladies project worked well for us.

Warwick Arts Centre has maintained a distinct policy, as an arts centre, of presenting the work of mainstream and experimental artists. This policy has been sustained and given the organisation a unique programme with broad appeal.

Keys to success are not for the fainthearted, demanding above all the desire to take risks and not abandoning programming experimental artists when the going gets tough. Audiences need consistency of programming and clear communication, especially with trailblazers / live art ambassadors.

The benefits are enormous. New artistic horizons, engaging performers and creators, excitement within the organisation about the extraordinary nature of some experimental work as well as press and TV attention for some of the more eyecatching work.

I can recommend the ride!

Alan Rivett is Director of Warwick Arts Centre, a large multi disciplinary venue based at the University of Warwick in Coventry. Alan started a career in theatre in the late 1960s at a tender age with the National Youth Theatre. In moments of rest he gravitated to the ICA, newly installed in the Mall for further excitement and never looked back. He has successfully steered Warwick Arts Centre programme to a position where it regularly hosts international theatre, music, visual arts and interdisciplinary events.
www.warwickartscentre.co.uk

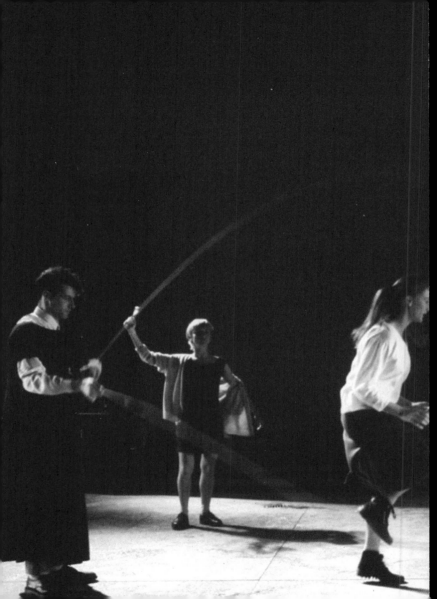

Growing Audiences

Veteran theatre PR Mark Borkowski, and the co-founders and former directors of the London International Festival of Theatre (LIFT), Rose Fenton and Lucy Neal, in conversation with journalist Brian Logan about the role of marketing in growing audiences for experimental theatre.

Brian Logan (BL)
Can you start by introducing your general principles of theatre marketing and publicity?

Mark Borkowski (MB)
Theatre is about changing people's lives. It's about exciting people. That's why I do this job. For me, as an individual with Polish roots, my greatest theatre experience was seeing *The Dead Class* by Tadeusz Kantor. This was in the 1970s, and I schlepped over to Riverside Studios to see it. Why? I was curious to discover what it was about. So I went, and I just couldn't believe what I saw. For days, there were images of that show in my mind. I thought: well, I'm touched by that, and I could easily never even have seen it. How less rich my life would have been!

Theatre marketing is about communicating that passion. Anybody who I work for, anybody who pays me a fee, knows that I am passionate about the work. Knows that I totally get their vision. And it becomes a mission for me, to take their work out there and get as many people as possible to see it. So that others can have the same feeling that I did when I saw Kantor. If a publicist hasn't got that kind of passionate commitment, if they're just doing a job for you – well, forget it.

To me, the essential questions that underpin theatre marketing are: what is interesting about the work? What are the visual pictures that will sell it, that will distil its impact? Who are the people likely to be excited by it, outside the traditional arts ghettoes? And answering these questions helps us create word-of-mouth. That's what theatre publicity is about.

BL
Is there scepticism towards marketing within theatre and the arts?

MB
The theatre critic Michael Coveney wrote in his book that I was evil for bringing modern marketing practises into theatre. Traditionally, theatre publicity was by rote: you got listings, you brought in a photographer for the previews, then you got the critics in. Job done. And there is still

a tendency to think that the review is all, that you're working towards the review. But the review is not all. The journey leading up to it is in itself very exciting. And crucial to the marketing of a production.

But theatre people aren't always sympathetic to that. I remember going to see an experimental theatre company in the East End of London, years and years ago. And the Artistic Director said to me, 'I've got to talk about marketing, because the Arts Council and the British Council and all the other funding bodies don't think we get enough audiences.' And I said, 'what do you mean?' And he said, 'well, we do it for our mates, really. If we get two people, that's good enough for us.' And I thought: how small an aspiration is that? But a lot of that old brigade felt that their primary duty was to the audience that were already committed to them.

So in the theatre, the publicist is usually the last person brought into the process. And by the time you're given the material, maybe you've only got three weeks to make it work. It's not enough. At the moment, I'm helping David Jubb, Artistic Director at Battersea Arts Centre (BAC) with an idea – and we've already been talking about it for two years.

BL
Could you talk about the specific challenges posed by marketing experimental performance? And can you relate that to your experiences working with LIFT?

MB
First of all, I don't think marketing experimental theatre is essentially different from marketing mainstream theatre. What you've got to look at is still: is the show good, or is it going to be good? That's really the only consideration.

BL
So, in terms of marketing, you don't see any reason why mainstream venues should be nervous of programming experimental work?

MB
No I don't.

Rose Fenton (RF)
I don't think mainstream venues are nervous anymore of alternative performance. In recent years, the major institutions have squatted on the ground of the fringe. The Barbican has the likes of Duckie and the artists William Yang and Richard Maxwell performing there. These are huge changes. There's even a case for saying experimental theatre has gone too mainstream, insofar as the media may now say to themselves: it's easy to hear about Bobby Baker, or the next generation of Bobby Bakers, through the Barbican and the National Theatre, rather than going out on a limb to some unknown, newly-emerging organisation.

In any event, I think labels are dangerous LIFT never sold itself as a festival of experimental theatre. We just said, 'this is amazing work from around the world, which will take you on an adventure, theatrically.' And that's how Mark led people into it.

MB
There's one sense in which contemporary performance is actually easier to sell. Because most of these companies are collectives of people with a vision, and with a real commitment to making their work. Look at Archaos: a collective of people together. The Jim Rose Circus: a collective of oddballs together. That's very important. The commitment of these people is their power. So marketing becomes about channelling that single-mindedness. The problem comes when that collective spirit becomes isolationist. Certain artists think 'the world is against us, they don't understand.' Better to think: we want the world to understand us. You need to understand and to find the types of people that will appreciate your work.

RF
When we first brought over De La Guarda – an unknown company, with no track record anywhere apart from Argentina – how did you sell them? What was your approach there?

MB

I travelled to Bordeaux to see De La Guarda, knowing nothing about the company. They performed in a nuclear submarine workshop. You went down, down, down into this room, which was dark like I'd never seen dark before. And silent like I'd never heard before. And then this performance happened. It was ecstasy. It was like a hallucinogenic drug. From that point onwards, a power and responsibility are passed onto you, to say 'I am determined to let everybody else experience what I've experienced.' Basically, that entails telling people, to their faces: 'you will enjoy this.'

That face-to-face communication is important. I used to have an office in Clerkenwell, and I used to take a handful of press releases across the road to The Guardian. And I would just walk in and talk to people. Publicity is about that connection. If you look people in the eyes and they can actually see or hear your enthusiasm, they get curious.

Lucy Neal (LN)

You arranged a press trip to Argentina for De La Guarda. That was quite shocking to us at the time, because LIFT's budget was not big – but you chose to invest our money in sending journalists overseas to see work in advance. Nowadays that's taken for granted. I was fascinated to read recently that Michael Billington had visited India – where he'd never been before – to see Tim Supple's *Midsummer Night's Dream*. And his review a few weeks later was qualitatively different, because he, as a human being, had engaged in the process of the making of the work.

In LIFT's case these trips were essential for the added reason that they led to preview articles. Our artists were often here for two or three days only, so we could never rely on reviews to sell tickets. Whatever coverage we received had to be something that captured people's imaginations at an earlier stage.

RF

Another benefit of the press trip is that it enables the participating writers to talk about the wider context: where is this work coming from? In Buenos Aires, post-dictatorship, there was a real sense of anarchy and questioning as a younger generation was making themselves heard. De La Guarda told us, 'we don't trust words anymore. We want to express ourselves through creating a new reality.' So with press trips, you can convey to your audience the context in which this work has happened.

MB
The key to press trips, and to promotion in general, is that you've got to find people who'll be interested. I have always, and I still do, read every newspaper every day. And what I have an ear for is, 'that writer might be interested in this.' It's about finding journalists with curious, interesting minds, regardless of their discipline, and matching them to the productions they might be interested in. Where things go wrong is if you just go, 'he is a theatre critic, let's send him.' You have to understand what these people are writing. Understand what they're interested in. And if they're not, don't force a square peg into a round hole.

But the publicist must go further. Why do art and entertainment have to get stuck in a ghetto? Why do they have to go on the arts pages? My mission has always been: how do you get work out of the ghetto and onto the pages where the most people are likely to see it?

LN
The thing I remember in terms of fresh approaches to getting audiences is that we worked with the Catalan artist, Alberto Vidal, whose LIFT'85 performances took place in London Zoo. Mark got Alberto onto the Terry Wogan show, which was a piece of live art in itself, and a genius piece of PR for his show.

MB
Alberto Vidal was a real battle, because when it came to marketing, London Zoo didn't want to know. My trick was to take a Daily Telegraph journalist called Byron Rogers along with me to a meeting at London Zoo. And he talked to the Zoo's director about how this was going to be the front page of the Telegraph magazine. That's how they started to recognise that this would be a big draw. Twenty thousand extra people went to London Zoo because of Vidal's show.

RF

I remember, Mark, every time we sat down to talk about an upcoming festival, your first question would always be: where are the images?

MB

One of the things I was noticing back then was the growing power of the image. There was more and more space for photos in newspapers. One of my first jobs was with a contemporary dance company. I sat down one day with them and said: 'the ideas you're coming up with, they'd make great pictures. Why don't you work with a photographer?' And they ummed and aahed and said, 'but we don't know what the show is going to be.' I encouraged them to introduce a photographer into their process, and the photos would help define the work, potentially. We got a part-photographer, part-artist called Holly Warburton and she created these amazing pictures. And magazines like ID and The Face, who hadn't seen theatre photos before, were running them across half-pages. I thought: we're onto something here. It's about distilling theatre – particularly visual theatre, and the types of theatre that have language barriers – into great images.

LN

I remember, Mark, images you got into Elle magazine. In the nineties, LIFT commissioned five new pieces of British work, and your task was to excite people about those commissions. You arranged five photo shoots for Elle with the five artists involved, including one of Bobby Baker hurling a pear across her kitchen into a wall for *Kitchen Show: One Dozen Kitchen Actions Made Public*. What did that achieve, do you think?

MB

You've got to seed the idea that something interesting is happening. And you seed that by choosing your publication. Basically, it's about trying to influence a group of people – not yet journalists and commissioning editors, that's the next stage. But with that project, you knew that if Elle was saying it, it became more likely that the Guardian might do something on it. Whereas, had I gone straight to the Guardian, there might have been a prejudice against covering it. So you go from stage to stage to stage, building and building.

That targeting process is essential. What happens now is that you get blanket coverage. In the old days, we sat at our desks with a pile of envelopes and a pile of press releases, and physically stuffed them in. So you would choose very carefully the people you'd address. Nowadays, the telephone and the email don't necessitate any selection process. You do too much, you contact too many people, and that's why we all get saturated and bored. In fact, all you need is one phone call to the right person at the right paper, and there'll be an explosion.

LN
New technologies can make the process harder. But they can also make it easier. I'm working on the Centenary Celebrations at the Tooting Bec Lido. Recently, two colleagues with an underwater camera took photographs of an artwork, at the bottom of the pool. Then they put the photograph on the image website Flickr, sent a press release out that afternoon, and the next day the picture and the whole press release was on the BBC website. I couldn't believe it: the whole thing, from conception to arriving on the BBC website in 24 hours. Totally DIY.

MB
It is exciting. With the democracy of the web and the reach of new communications technologies, it's incredible what you can achieve. And you can deploy more tools than ever to generate an audience for experimental work in particular. But if you go back to the principles of good publicity, they have not changed. The same methods were used by the promoters of the Roman forum through to Barnum and beyond. Everybody has curiosity. The technology is more sophisticated, but we're still driven by the same human emotions. Which goes back to what I said earlier: you have to be passionate, you have to believe. Nothing changes, really: contact and relationships remain.

Mark Borkowski is in his late forties in circus years, suffers from bouts of pathological storytelling, and as a result is forced to invent himself every five years. His passport currently states his occupation as shibboleth of spin, but has included ringmaster and dream merchant.

Rose Fenton is an independent arts producer, writer and advisor. Co Founder/Director of the London International Festival of Theatre (LIFT) with Lucy Neal from 1981–2005 and author of *The Turning World*, she is currently working in Europe and the Middle East on a range of projects within contemporary performance, as well as training to be a yoga teacher.

Brian Logan is a freelance arts writer, a former assistant theatre editor of Time Out London and the comedy critic of The Guardian. He is a founder member, deviser and performer with Cartoon de Salvo theatre company. He currently has a play in development with the National Theatre of Scotland Workshop.

Lucy Neal is an independent arts producer, writer and broadcaster. Co-founder/director of the London International Festival of Theatre (LIFT), with Rose Fenton, from 1981–2005 and author of *The Turning World*, she is currently Research Fellow at the University of Winchester on The Mary Neal Project. She is also a celebrant, a cold-water swimming champ and mother of four.

BITE, Artsadmin and Duckie swap notes. Louise Jeffreys and Toni Racklin from the Barbican talk to Judith Knight of Artsadmin, Simon Casson from Duckie, and Daniel Brine of the Live Art Development Agency about BITE (Barbican International Theatre Events); its role in the theatre landscape, development of artists, and the changing nature of practice.

Louise Jeffreys (LJ)

The first BITE season was in 1998. It was the brainchild of the Barbican's Artistic Director Graham Sheffield and was informed by the Royal Shakespeare Company's decision not to continue to occupy the Barbican theatres all year-round, and research which identified that a gap in the London market was international theatre, particularly of a large scale.

By the end of the 1990s a lot of international work had been presented in London. We would never ever claim to be the first: LIFT was obviously extremely important, places like the Lyric Hammersmith frequently presented international work, and the National Theatre had international seasons. We benefited from situations that others made. But there hadn't been somewhere with a large stage that presented international work on such a regular basis and perhaps still isn't with the focus on performance that we have.

For BITE we have two theatres, the 1,100 seat main house and The Pit which is anything from about 100 – 180 seats depending on the formation. The context for these spaces is the arts centre, which also helps because alongside us we have cinemas, galleries and a concert hall, so there are opportunities on occasion for cross-fertilisation and festivals that take in all of those different spaces and genres.

Within our focus on large scale international performance a lot of the work crosses boundaries and mixes genres, and we're not restricted by any particular box of dance or drama or music or anything, so we're completely free to look across every genre, and I think that is one of the situations that has been most important to us.

We do present British companies but what's absolutely true of the British companies we've presented is all of them have an international life. So it isn't the international companies *and* the British companies, it's the international companies of which some are British.

Similarly, in BITE we don't make distinctions between the different types of work we do – it isn't a case of 'oh we better take a risk on some experimental stuff.' We feel that we provide a theatre context in which experimental work can happen. But for us we just don't see a big difference between the most conservative work and the most experimental work that we do.

Judith Knight (JK)
One of the manifestations of your attitude is the BITE brochure, which seems to give equal weight to all productions, for instance Deborah Warner's *Julius Caesar* gets as much prominence as does something in The Pit. I think showing the work together in that context and demonstrating to your audiences that the programme is seen as a whole is incredibly important for both the smaller scale and the British work.

Toni Racklin (TR)
And that's very deliberate. It also reflects our own positioning, how we view our work. A show that comes in for half an hour in The Pit is as important and as valuable to us as a show that's going to run six weeks in the main house, because we all have to put the same amount of work into it – in administration, marketing, press – everything is of the same value and hopefully that is reflected in the brochure.

We always use our programmes and our website to say; 'well you're here for this, how about that? How about this one?' Where there are some parallels and some links into experimental work we very much want people to move out of what they would naturally come to and to see something else as well. People are trusting us – they'll look in the brochure, they'll see there's a multi-buy scheme and they'll book for shows they'd go to naturally and then also take in something else.

Daniel Brine (DB)
So, it is a long term investment? Perhaps if Duckie's *C'est Barbican* had been presented totally out of context and not built into a long term plan, the audiences would not have come, and you are clearly interested in gaining the trust of audiences.

TR
We don't want a hit and run approach.

DB

And this implies developing relationships with companies as well as audiences?

LJ

Yes, and what works for us is when the artist or company and BITE both have a purpose. It has got to mean something to both of us. We have got to have a function and the artist or the company need to get something out of being here and when that comes together – which it often does by chance – then it really works.

TR

With Duckie it was actually synchronicity because we had been running a cabaret strand called *The Velvet Lounge* and then (as if by magic) we heard of this thing in this seedy pub in South London that I was so terrified to walk into that I had to be escorted in! And it was like … 'oh yes this is it, of course, this is it.' And it was a marriage of the moment because it was a natural development for us and answered our remit, while at the same time Duckie had developed over many years and had a very strong following so it was a great chance to put strong work into a new context. So, we were transposing them here and we made The Pit their home. It wasn't just plonking them in here, we had to create this environment that felt absolutely spot on, which was in itself a big ask. The next show we did together has a whole different set of challenges, for instance serving food within a show, and we had to address these things. We had to involve the box office, the front of house, the technical team, to ensure everyone at the Barbican embraced this and made it a very smooth and very sharp operation.

Simon Casson (SC)

It was amazing how the audience changed when we came here – I've never seen so many straight people in my life all in one room together! And that's really interesting for us, so the audience became 50/50 straight/gay and it really burst us out of our bubble and our ghetto. For us, it was great.

JK

The same happened with Bobby Baker because she had performed a lot and had a huge following already before she came to the Barbican. Originally, she did The Pit for three weeks, and that built an audience. I knew by looking at the audience, and we do know from the Barbican's statistics, that many of the audience saw Bobby for the first time in The Pit. Bobby had always had a festival / visual arty / experimental theatre audience before – a LIFT audience – but after three weeks in The Pit there was an opportunity to present work on the main stage.

LJ

Because we realised there was a big and growing audience there, and that Bobby hadn't previously done a large scale piece. So we tried Bobby on the main stage and that sold beyond all of our expectations. In fact, Duckie and Bobby Baker are two of the artists that we present that do very well at the box office – it's not a worry in that sense.

DB

So there's obviously fantastic benefits for the artist to come here, in terms of increasing audiences, but presumably there's a similar benefit for the Barbican in terms of introducing new audiences to the Barbican through these artists?

LJ

Absolutely! And expanding the reach of what we do.

DB

It's important to acknowledge that from the experimental theatre sector's point of view the absolutely important role the Barbican plays in presenting work to new audiences. There are some things that only a venue of the scale of the Barbican can do – such as extended runs or presenting work on larger stages. And its very important in terms of the ecology of experimental practices that there are places like Duckie at the Vauxhall Tavern or Battersea Arts Centre (BAC) which can put on the first shows of practitioners working in more experimental ways. The artists can try out their ideas, they can develop them, then tour them around the country. Ultimately, there may be an opportunity to show the work in a venue like the Barbican but its important to see the smaller experimental venues working in partnership. It might not be co-commissioning but in terms of the ecology it's a very important role that Barbican plays.

LJ

And its informal. Certainly with Ridiculusmus, the relationship with BAC and David Jubb has been extremely important. We began by presenting one of their works then we presented two together. Next time we'll hopefully present their films, do talks, panel discussions and present some of the older pieces as well so that we begin to have a critical focus on the work – something slightly different than just presenting.

SC

We should just be really clear about this, you're talking about performance that's experimental. Experimental performance by its very nature can fail. You can have a total flop. Because this is experimental theatre practice, some die on their arse and some are the most wonderful things you ever see.

DB

That's why a commitment from presenters to the long-haul is important. So that if something fails the next thing may not. It's also why different understandings of risk and nurturing risk are important. It's important that artists are able to develop their work out of the heat of the spotlight – that's the risk of the Duckies and BACs. Barbican's risk is very different, it is putting that type of work on this type of scale to this level of audience.

SC

And there are examples of how *not* to do it. One promoter put us on because the Barbican and the Sydney Opera House had put us on. You get this sense that some promoters or producers don't really know what they are dealing with! And they don't understand the need to think differently and perhaps creatively about all their business – from marketing to front of house. We did about 60 shows at the Barbican and every single one sold out, because they look after you and because they know what they are doing. But, you can't just put something on and cross your fingers, you need to know what you're dealing with and work to get it right.

DB

In a publication called *Towards 2010: New Times, New Challenges For The Arts*, Robert Hewison wrote that 'traditional buildings that present the arts will have to adapt to demands both from artists and audiences to rewrite their spaces.' Does this ring true for you – both the artist and the venues? And if so, what can 'adaptation' and 'rewriting' mean practically?

LJ

Well, I suppose we try and do it, which I think is the most important thing. I think there is still a real need for the umbrella organisations like Dance Umbrella and LIFT – those festival organisations which are not building-based and which say, quite rightly, that one of the benefits for them is that they can choose the right space for the right work. Our role is to work with the two spaces we have. Our production team bend-over backwards from our constant demands; try and put a new auditorium in the main theatre, bring the main stage out, or change the seating in The Pit in a million different ways. Our job here is to programme these spaces and we try and be as flexible with them as we can but there's a limit beyond which we can't go.

JK

It's not just about getting theatres to take more risks, it is also about encouraging audiences to experience something new, and then to like it and in the end expect it. And its not just about replacing the mainstream, it is more about infiltrating it, so that boundaries get narrower and experimental work is no longer put into a 'weird and wonderful' box, but is strong and leading the way, for everything else to follow.

DB

Hewison suggests that audiences are demanding a re-write of our cultural spaces. Do you get a sense that audiences are seeking out different types of experiences which might go beyond the traditional theatrical spaces?

LJ

Absolutely, I think so, but the changing interests and attitudes of audiences are not matched in journalism and that's a huge problem. When we want someone to write about BITE; someone might write about the theatre, someone might write about the dance, someone might mention the operas we've done or music theatre. But whenever we try and think about someone who might write about all of BITE we find that very hard because newspapers have divided specialisms like opera, dance and theatre. In the Observer this week for Mark Morris' ENO production of *King Arthur* there was a big page and it used the word 'hybrid' but the dance critic had written about the dance part and in a box at the bottom the music critic had written about the music part – as if they were two completely different things! This needs to develop.

One development is that audiences are writing their own 'crits' on these new websites that are emerging. Its not big yet but I think it will be, and I think more and more people will want to write their own comments and let other people – other audiences – know about their experiences.

SC

And those experiences are important because they'll change your life. We'll remember them. I went to the Village Gate in New York in 1993 and saw Penny Arcade – they turned the lights out and Quentin Crisp spoke quietly and Marianne Faithful came on in-between the scenes singing the *Ballad of Lucy Jordan* and I had the time of my life! And I want to work with you lot and do that for other people. It's important to me.

DB

The changing of our lives, the activating of our lives – is there something that experimental work can do especially? Why would we invest in experimental work with all its difficulties and its challenges?

TR

Because it taps into new parts of us, and stretches us in new ways.

JK
Because it can change your way of thinking. Its imagination, its looking at the world in a different way.

TR
You might know what you are going to get from a production of Shakespeare – however, fine it is – its kind of known but then something else – something new – can just shift you slightly.

LJ
It's that thought when you're seeing a show – even when you see shows as much as I do – 'my God I'd never have thought of that.' And that's that sort of wow moment when you see or think of something which has never struck you before. Those are the most exciting moments.

DB
Simon, didn't your marketing once say 'Demolish the Theatre', shouldn't the Barbican be scared of you?

SC
Well, I personally don't believe in The Theatre. I don't believe in the proscenium arch, I don't believe in the stalls. I want to take a baseball bat and smash them all up – I'm not interested in them, I'd set fire to them. I want to do something else. I just have this passion, and it's a lifelong passion and it's for performance – I call it performance. Now that touches on this thing called live art, it touches on this thing which is called theatre. I'd rather do it on the roof.

We are the modern world. We're not trying to understand someone else, we're fucking 'it'. I'm 40 this year, but I'm still 'it'. And the reason why I think this conversation is so important is because theatre needs to be revolutionary, ever-changing. Even bloody crappy telly ever-changes. Telly is very different now than it was ten years ago and performance culture has to change constantly too. That's why this notion of experimental in the mainstream isn't a question of 'should it happen?' But it's 'why isn't it happening and why isn't it happening faster?'

Simon Casson is the producer for Duckie. Defining post gay culture at the start of the century, Duckie is an independent arts outfit producing a mix of cultural interventions, nightclubs, new mode pop and arty performance events, and anti-theatre ridiculum.
www.duckie.co.uk

Louise Jeffreys is Head of Theatre at the Barbican, responsible since 1999 for BITE (Barbican International Theatre Events). Prior to the Barbican, Louise's previous roles include Administrative Director at the Nottingham Playhouse, Head of Production at Bayerische Staatsoper, Munich, and Technical Director at the English National Opera.
www.barbican.org.uk

Judith Knight is the founder and Director of Artsadmin which for 27 years has supported experimental and interdisciplinary arts projects. It established Toynbee Studios as a centre for the development of new work, with an advisory and bursary scheme with residencies, showcases and performances. Artsadmin produces the work of many artists including Bobby Baker.
www.artsadmin.co.uk

The **Live Art Development Agency** offers a portfolio of Resources, Professional Development Schemes, Projects and Initiatives for the support and development of Live Art practices and discourses in London, the UK and internationally. The Agency is committed to working strategically, in partnership, and in consultation with artists and organisations in the cultural sector.
www.thisisLiveArt.co.uk

Toni Racklin joined the Barbican in 1996 to launch BITE. As Administrative Producer, she works closely with Louise Jeffreys on the realisation of the BITE yearly programme. Before joining the Barbican, she worked with a diverse range of companies including; the Round House, the Royal Court, Lyric Hammersmith, Women's Playhouse Trust, Liverpool Playhouse and Festival d'Aix en Provence.
www.barbican.org.uk

Theatre, at its most radically distinctive, is the place where people gather together to invent their future. Consequently, experimentation is its only viable practice: not merely a training ground, not a marginal self-involvement, but theatre fully and faithfully encountering itself in public. It's hard to imagine a more vital optimism.

Chris Goode

Making
Smaller

Keith Khan talks to Lois Keidan
of the Live Art Development
Agency about his approaches
as artistic director of the ground
breaking company motiroti, and
his two years as CEO of
London's Rich Mix.

Lois Keidan (LK)

Wearing your artist's hat let's start by talking about the ways in which artists can influence audience development and the nature of cultural institutions. In particular motiroti's *Moti Roti Puttli Chunni* (1993) at Theatre Royal Stratford East and the creation and touring of *Alladeen* (2003). How did the relationship with Theatre Royal begin?

Keith Khan (KK)

After motiroti completed site specific productions of *Flying Costumes, Floating Tombs* (1991) we were looking for a theatre venue for a new project that aimed to restage an Indian movie on stage, using all the tropes and facets of what happens in Bollywood. I was interested in the work of Philip Hedley, Artistic Director of Theatre Royal Stratford East because he was very focused on audience development and had built an audience that was clearly not the kind of audience that other venues had. It seemed that the way Theatre Royal approached marketing and audience development was as important as their actual productions, and I thought that they would be a good fit for our own aspirations for this project. When I approached Philip Hedley, he not only agreed to house the project, but also to invest in it. The piece itself was a fairly conventional piece of narrative theatre – or rather it *looked* like a fairly conventional piece of narrative theatre – so it worked within Theatre Royal's structures. *Moti Roti Puttli Chunni* was a success and out of this we went on to do another piece with Theatre Royal, *One Night* (1997) but by then motiroti had dumped the conventional theatre model based on having the writer at the top of a hierarchy, and had instigated a much more collaborative model in which it was understood that the person doing the music, or the person doing the lighting, had as much to contribute to the creation of a theatre environment as anyone else involved.

LK

And how did that work for Theatre Royal? Was it a big shake-up for them to have to deal with the production of that kind of collaborative model?

KK

Well, it was all very different from what they normally did but they were really supportive and willing to take the risk. And of course they were committed to audience development and recognised that there weren't enough Asian audiences in the UK.

LK

So their strategy (as a venue and through their collaboration with you) was not about trying to persuade Asian audiences to come and see something they might not necessarily be interested in, but rather to try to create work that those audiences could be interested in.

KK

Exactly. It was about changing the programme and therefore changing the audience.

LK

I remember standing in the queue for *Moti Roti Puttli Chunni* at Theatre Royal and the man in front of me warning his friends that Keith Khan's work was 'a little bit weird'. I've always been intrigued as to whether he and his friends would have come to see the work if it hadn't been at Theatre Royal.

KK

I think the venue made a difference to the audiences we attracted. The other big difference was that Nitish Bharawaj who played Krishna in one of India's biggest soaps, The Mahabarata, was in the show. Working with someone who was not from a theatre background was great, because he brought with him a cinematic way of performing and acting that contributed enormously to the concept of the piece.

LK

So motiroti's strategy was about bringing together different approaches and practices and putting them together as something that 'looked like theatre' within a theatre.

KK

The strange thing is that we were absolutely committed to making *Moti Roti Puttli Chunni* in the way that Indian film was made – recreating in minute detail all of those effects like tracking shots and close ups and the kind of interplay between screen and stage. I think that if we hadn't approached it so seriously and intensely it would have just been another piece of theatre.

LK

But it was still a fantastic night out *in* a theatre. One of the other things I remember from that night was that you had a great cliff-hanger before the interval where the murderer was revealed in Hindi but not English, so in the toilets during the interval there were all these women begging the Hindi speakers to tell them who the murderer was. This brought a dynamic to the theatre experience, and an energy to the venue, that I've rarely experienced.

KK

One of the things about the Theatre Royal audience is that they have a lot of energy, and are far from passive. But the touring of *Moti Roti Puttli Chunni* to theatres in the UK and internationally was horrible because the venues didn't have the same commitment to audience development and were not able to attract Asian audiences. Even if they did bring in different audiences, they often did not have the generosity or vision to make those audiences feel welcome or comfortable. We had so many conversations with venues in which we'd say: if people come with their own food let them in, and if people come late let them in because we don't mind, the cast don't mind and in fact it'll benefit the show – a bit of rustling at the beginning is good. But the venues were rarely interested in such conversations.

LK

So, Theatre Royal were able to break their own systems, to accommodate different ways of working – both artistically and with audiences – and other venues were resistant and that showed in their audiences?

KK

Yes.

LK

Alladeen was a different model. It was a collaboration with The Builders Association, an interdisciplinary theatre company from New York, and was in many ways an even more conventional piece of theatre.

KK

Ali Zaidi of motiroti and I had seen The Builders Association's *Jet Lag* at the Barbican in London, which combined visual narrative and cinematic imagery with theatre in ways I hadn't seen before and so I proposed a collaboration to Marianne Weems, the company's director and one of the leading theatre and technology directors in the world. What's different about the way that The Builders Association work is not only that their pieces are more rooted in theatrical traditions but they also involve co-producers at a very early stage. So from the outset of our collaboration – even before we had a writer onboard – there were four co-producers all of whom were taking risks and making an investment in the piece: Barbican, London; Wexner Centre, Columbus Ohio; Walker Arts Centre, Minneapolis; and Museum of Contemporary Art, Chicago. The piece evolved over a two year period through workshop sessions supported by the four initial co-producers and then we hired a space to try out aspects of the piece and to invite other producing venues to see where the work was at and to give us feedback. I think this opening up of the process is a good way of working because either further investment comes in or you realise that you need to change the piece. I suppose you have to have sensitive producers that appreciate seeing work at a fairly rough stage, but for me to be actually directly collaborating with the venues from such an early stage is a great model.

LK

The producers that you're talking about were venue managers, not independent producers, and I imagine it is a really good model for them as well. Possibly one of the challenges for venue managers of such different ways of making theatre is that there aren't necessarily any 'givens' – there isn't a script, and there isn't a design you can look at to let you know how its going to work in your space. Because of the process-based way of making experimental theatre its difficult for venue managers to know in advance what it will be like, and this makes it even more high risk. But in the model you're proposing they are part of the process: directly involved in the creation of the piece and better equipped and informed to produce and promote the work within their own distinct contexts.

KK

Yes, those rehearsals and development periods were really crucial, and the input of those venues was important in terms of moving the production on.

LK

I remember at the time you and Marianne Weems of The Builders Association saying that one of the things about the collaboration was that it was not just an artistic marriage but that it enabled The Builders Association to access your (Asian) audiences, and enabled motiroti to access white middle class venues that would otherwise have been resistant. Did that work for both of you?

KK

Yes, it worked successfully all round. I think the door opening to the Barbican main house wouldn't have happened without The Builders Association. They helped the scaling up of the project and of motiroti, and likewise we helped broker the relationship with the Brooklyn Academy of Music which has ended up with them co-producing the company's next piece.

LK

Lets move on from motiroti to your taking on the role of Chief Executive Officer (CEO) of Rich Mix from 2004 to 2006. With that role you were wearing a very different hat but you still had the same cultural values. I would be interested in you talking about the ways in which you were positioning Rich Mix to be able to respond to notions of experimentation. How were you developing the building to meet the needs of new practices and new ways of working, and as somewhere that had a different set of cultural values from more rarefied and exclusive arts venues?

KK

It's very clear what my contribution to Rich Mix was: I created it as a house of process. Rich Mix has become a place where you can see work as it's being made and see artists trying things out. One of the things we instigated is the public studio with a window on to the street which will always have some kind of activity in it. My idea was to create an open cultural model that allows people in – that is about opening up process, about artists inviting people in to their work at different stages.

LK

And why do you think that's important?

KK

Well, because the first thing we tried was a static exhibition and I realised that it didn't really make sense for that building, or for its staff or even for the artists because the art seemed fossilised. Those tropes of the visual arts world are very powerful, but they didn't work in a new type of space as they are too passive. Coming to see this exhibition was a bit like going into a museum rather than a lively cultural place. On reflection what seemed to be important was when there was loads of kids and young men hanging around Leepu, the artist from Bangladesh we had invited to transform a non-status car into a super swish sports car. The audiences were actively engaging with what was going on, and we thought that maybe we didn't need passive pre-packaged exhibitions and could just invest in process itself.

But I was also looking at how outcomes and products from these processes can be packaged and produced and taken out of the building. I hoped that we might be able to evolve work at Rich Mix that would be of sufficient quality to end up on the main stage of the Barbican and in a way this follows the motiroti models.

I also think it is important for Rich Mix and other new cultural institutions to prioritise areas of culture that are less rarefied or restricted. So, I was not prioritising visual art because there are so many galleries in the East End of London and because we shouldn't be clogging up our spaces with the brokering of artists into galleries.

Likewise with theatre. There are a lot of theatres out there and the work that Rich Mix presents should always be much more experimental, more risky, more politically engaged, and more concerned with audiences. So at Rich Mix we developed a set of Dogme-like rules – criteria by which we accept projects. We asked ourselves: Does it have political ramifications? Is it helping audience development? For us this was a really good way to think about how we develop both art for the future and audiences for the future.

LK

One of the exciting things about you, your work, and where you're heading is that you are looking at Culture rather than Art, and that you are blurring distinctions between restricted art and popular art, and setting different sorts of cultural values. And the fact that Rich Mix was not an existing building changing its artistic policy, but that you were starting it from scratch means that it could have the potential to be a unique and exciting model for the UK.

KK

Yes, I think it's a unique model. If you look around the world the models for new cultural institutions are limited because many of them are aimed at relatively minority markets and are preoccupied with economics – the visual arts world is certainly about economics and even the theatrical one to some degree. But there's a lot of important and exciting stuff happening that is on one hand more experimental and on the other more accessible, and that is developing new cultural models, and there just aren't the kind of places for that. But having spent two years shaping that vision and creating local jobs at Rich Mix I've now moved on.

LK

Finally, can you talk about the importance of investing in different ways of working and the necessity of taking risks. Why shouldn't we play it safe?

KK

There's a danger at the moment because audiences seem to be diminishing but actually they're just changing. Audiences have changed almost unrecognisably in the last ten years and the way that people engage with culture is fundamentally different now. The online component – the idea of user-generated content – is really critical now. The kind of public interface that technology gives means that even work that is 'minority' on a local level can reach 'majority' audiences globally who are interested in the same ideas. So, the future has got to be about making smaller and actually being more specialised, rather than becoming more generalist, because that's the kind of curse that we're seeing around us – a bland environment of safe culture, which is destined for mass appeal. I believe what's being missed is that if you invest in the edges you're going to end up with a much more vibrant fall out.

Keith Khan is an artist whose career has involved working with communities and technology to engage with diverse audiences and practices. His work is large scale and celebratory and uses the energy of popular culture. He was a carnivalist for many years and has been involved in national cultural projects including *Celebration Commonwealth*, for the Queen's Jubilee Parade in 2002. Keith was a co-founder of **motiroti** and Chief Executive Officer of Rich Mix from 2004 to 2006. Keith is a Board member of Platform for Art, chairs the Diversity Panel of the DCMS Creative Economy programme and is a member of Council at Arts Council England.

The **Live Art Development Agency** offers a portfolio of Resources, Professional Development Schemes, Projects and Initiatives for the support and development of Live Art practices and discourses in London, the UK and internationally. The Agency is committed to working strategically, in partnership, and in consultation with artists and organisations in the cultural sector.
www.thisisLiveArt.co.uk

Further reading

An eclectic selection suggested by the Programme Notes contributors.

Judith Helmer and Florian Malzacher (eds).
Not Even a Game Anymore: the Theatre of Forced Entertainment.
Alexander Verlag Berlin, 2004.

John Fox.
Eyes on Stalks.
A & C Black, 2003.

Tim Etchells.
Endland Stories.
PULP Faction, 1998.

Rose de Wend Fenton and Lucy Neal.
The Turning World, Stories from the London International Festival of Theatre.
Calouste Gulbenkian Foundation, 2005.

Mark Borkowski (ed).
Improperganda: The Art of the Publicity Stunt
Vision On Publishing, 2000.

Nicky Childs and Jeni Walwyn (eds).
A Split Second of Paradise: Live Art, Installation and Performance.
Rivers Oram Press, 1998.

Maria Shevtsova.
Dodin and the Maly Drama Theatre.
Routledge, 2004.

Carl Miller.
Stages of Desire: Male and Female Homosexuality in British and American Theatre.
Cassell, 1999.

David Savran.
The Wooster Group, 1975–1985: Breaking the Rules.
Umi Research Pr (August 1986)

Philip Auslander.
Liveness.
Taylor and Francis, 2005.

Ritsaert ten Cate and Mike Figgis.
Ritsaert ten Cate – Man Looking for Words.
Theater Instituut Nederland, 1996.

Neil Bartlett.
What Mainstream? in It's Queer Up North 1992–1996: A Catalogue of Queer Performance.
It's Queer Up North, 1996.

Lapine.
Mickery Pictorial 1965–1987. Theatre Communications Group, 1988.

Richard Benson.
Night Fever: Club Writing in "The Face", 1980–1996.
Pan Macmillan, 1997.

Guillermo Gomez-Pena.
Ethno-Techno.
Routledge, 2005.

Greil Marcus.
LIPSTICK TRACES, A Secret History of the 20th Century.
Harvard University Press, 1989.

David Vaughan, Merce Cunningham.
Fifty Years.
Aperture 1997.

Georges Perec.
Species of Spaces and Other Pieces.
Penguin, 1998.

Adrian Heathfield (ed).
Live: Art and Performance.
Tate Publishing, 2004.

Jon Savage.
England's Dreaming: Anarchy, Sex Pistols, Punk Rock, and Beyond.
St. Martin's Griffin, 2002.

Peter Brook.
The Empty Space.
Penguin, 1990.

Programme Notes
Case studies for locating experimental theatre

Programme Notes is a collaboration between the Live Art Development Agency and Arts Council England that has been created as part of a strategy to strengthen the infrastructure for experimental work and develop new and high profile contexts for contemporary practices.

The Live Art Development Agency is committed to supporting a diverse range of artists working in a broad range of live contexts and to bringing concepts of interdisciplinary practice and collaboration to the foreground.
www.thisisLiveArt.co.uk

Arts Council England is committed to experimentation and the development of new audiences for new work. Through its Theatre Policy it continues to place a particular emphasis on experimental and interdisciplinary practice and is keen to further embed new work within the fabric of the theatre buildings it funds.
www.artscouncil.org.uk

Edited by Daniel Brine and Lois Keidan.

First Published 2007 by the Live Art Development Agency.

ISBN: 0-9546040-4-0.

Contributions © individual contributors.

Design by pkmb.

Programme Notes is available to buy through Unbound, an online shop for Live Art books and dvds.
www.thisisUnbound.co.uk

The Editors thank all the contributors, David Micklem, Adrian Heathfield, Andrew Mitchelson, Robert Pacitti, and Sheila Ghelani

Live Art
Development
Agency

Photo Credits.
Cover: Ursula Martinez, *Show Off*.
Photo Hugo Glendinning.

P 1: Duckie, *C'est Barbican!*
Photo Hugo Glendinning.

P 4: Gob Squad, *Calling Laika*.
Photo Simon Cunningham.

P 11: Kira O'Reilly, *Untitled Action for Bomb Shelter Kuopio*.
ANTI – Contemporary Art Festival 2003, Kuopio, Finland.
Photo Pekka Mäkinen.

P 18, 24 and 30: Empty Stages: Venice, Brussels and Ghent.
Photo Hugo Glendinning and Tim Etchells.

P 37: Julian Clary in Jean Genet's *Splendid's* translated, designed and directed by Neil Bartlett, Lyric Hammersmith London 1995.
Photo John Haynes.

P 38: Anita Dobson, Guy Dartnell, Amanda Harris and Gregor Trutor in Marivaux's *The Island of Slaves*, translated designed and directed by Neil Bartlett, Lyric Hammersmith 2002.

P 46: Station House Opera, *Black Works*. Photo: Steve Whitson.

P 57 and 59: SKID 180.
Photo Joel Chester Fildes.

P 66: Marisa Carnesky, *Carnesky's Ghost Train*.
Photo courtesy the artist.

P 72: Graeme Miller, *A Girl Skipping*.
Photo Bob van Dantzig.

P 82: Bobby Baker, *How to Live*.
Photo Andrew Whittuck.

P 94: motiroti and The Builders Association, *Alladeen*.
Photo Simone Lynn.

Inside back cover: Martin Freeman as Buttons in *Cinderella*, devised by Improbable Theatre with Neil Bartlett, Lyric Hammersmith 1999.
Photo John Haynes.

Financially assisted by Arts Council England.

Over the last twenty years I have been working as a performer and director crossing between the worlds of experimental and mainstream theatre. Surprisingly it has been this diversity of influence which I think has made Improbable's work both challenging and POPULAR! In that time it has been essential to let the experimental work feed the work we've done in the mainstream. I learnt as much about tragedy from Rose English and performing at the Comedy Store as I did from directing shows at the Rep theatres. It is essential for the mainstream to acknowledge the debt it has to those working outside the traditional structures and that doesn't just mean giving them a gig and then moving on! It is essential to invest in the process of nurturing the work and develop a muscle for holding that particular space in which this work can grow in.

Phelim McDermott,
Artistic Director, Improbable